LOVE
FROM
WALES

In memory of Emrys James, actor.

LOVE
FROM
WALES

AN ANTHOLOGY

EDITED BY
TONY CURTIS & SIÂN JAMES

SEREN BOOKS

Seren is the book imprint of
Poetry Wales Press Ltd
Nolton Street, Bridgend, Wales
www.seren-books.com

ISBN 1-85411-067-5
First published in 1991
Reprinted 1995, 2005, 2008, 2009

A CIP record for this title is available from
the British Library

The publisher works with the financial assistance
of the Welsh Books Council

Printed by Bell & Bain Ltd, Glasgow

CONTENTS

SPRING

SUMMER

AUTUMN

WINTER

SPRING

To Morfudd

Who made an ache under my rib
whom I love and have loved
whose colour God made
whose forehead's a white flower
to whom God gave red gold
her hair a tongue of gold
her neck of straight growth
her breasts full spheres
two scarlet sunny cheeks
her brows of London black
her eyes bright enclosures
her nose of a sweet girl.
Her smile the five delights
her body takes me from God.

Anon., 15th century

The Heart of a Dreamer

I broke my heart in five pieces
And buried a part by the sea,
And I hid a part in the mountains
And the third in the root of a tree,
And the fourth I gave to a singer
Who shared his wild ecstasy,
But the best I gave to a woman
Who gave all her heart to me.

Idris Davies

13

from: *How Green was my Valley*

'Would you marry me, Huw?' she asked, very shy, with a look sideways, and a small voice.

'No,' I said , 'there is dull you are, girl. Not from school yet, and marry?'

'My mother married from school,' she said, 'and four of us still home, and me the youngest, and like a sister instead of Mama. Let us be married, Huw, and have a little house, is it?'

'To hell, girl,' I said, ' I will have to earn before marrying.'

'Come to work with my father,' Ceinwen said, and came nearer. 'Learn the business while you are working and have good wages, then we can marry and have our own little house, is it?'

'Look you,' I said, 'no more silliness, to-night. To hear the nightingales we came up here. So listen.'

'Well, give me a kiss, then,' she said.

'Go from here,' I said, and put more tart in my mouth. 'Nightingales, not marrying, or kissing.'

'Speaking with the mouth full,' she said. 'There is manners for you.'

'Leave me to eat in peace,' I said.

'I wish I had cooked nothing,' she said, and angry. 'You would be starving.'

'We would have gone from here the sooner, then,' I said, and glad to have a change of subject.

'O, Huw,' she said, and pulling her handkerchief from her belt, 'there is nasty you are to me.'

And she cried.

With her legs curling under her, and hidden in the white-ness of her dress, and her hair like new hay fallen about her and spreading on the grass, and the white handkerchief in both her hands pressed to her eyes almost hidden among her hair, and her voice coming in little swords of sound at the end of each breath, O, there is a soreness inside me now, to re-member Ceinwen as she cried up there on the mountain and the nightingales sang about us, and the firelight was bright upon her, for the fire is out, the nightingales are quiet, and she has gone.

Richard Llewellyn

from: *In Praise of a Girl*

Moon of Wales, your loveliness prevails.
Your praise and glory, peerless girl,
now impel me to applaud
your sweet looks, your subtle tongue,
dawn-sweet dearest, purest, prettiest, many-beautied,
unpolluted and reputed spotless rose.
There's none to make comparison,
wave sparkling in the darkling,
with your parabling of sweet peace,
piece of goodness, fond enchantress, blithesome dove,
lucent, laughing, blameless slip of love.

Huw Morus, 17th century
(tr. Gwyn Williams)

Spring

Now open flowers on the shirts of boys;
now mica glistens, asphalt's morning dew,
from pavements up. Now all the girls look pregnant,
and small red sports cars blossom on the roads.

Now all birds are not sparrows; now all women
unwrap their shapes from winter. Now the man
who thought it might be fun to walk to work
finds all sight aches, all touch troubles his blood.

Now all the state of opening, upspring, bud's
soft burst, a green grenade, scrapes at his grief;
now all the many dead dress him in black
for what they had and what he cannot keep.

Sheenagh Pugh

from: A Prospect of the Sea

Her mouth was an inch from his. Her long fore-fingers touched his eyelids. This is a story, he said to himself, about a boy on holiday kissed by a broom-rider; she flew from a tree on to a hill that changes its size like a frog that loses its temper; she stroked his eyes and put her chest against him; and when she had loved him until he died she carried him off inside her to a den in a wood. But the story, like all stories, was killed as she kissed him; now he was a boy in a girl's arms, and the hill stood above a true river, and the Jarvis peaks and their trees towards England were as Jarvis had known them when he walked there with his lovers and horses for half a century, a century ago.

Who had been frightened of a wind out of the light swelling the small country? The piece of a wind in the sun was like the wind in an empty house; it made the corners mountains and crowded the attics with shadows who broke through the roof; through the country corridors it raced in a hundred voices, each voice larger than the last, until the last voice tumbled down and the house was full of whispers.

'Where do you come from?' she whispered in his ear. She took her arms away but still sat close, one knee between his legs, one hand on his hands. Who had been frightened of a sunburned girl no taller or stranger than the pale girls at home who had babies before they were married?

'I come from Amman valley,' said the boy.

'I have a sister in Egypt,' she said, 'who lives in a pyramid...' She drew him closer.

'They're calling me in for tea,' he said.

She lifted her frock to her waist.

Dylan Thomas

Welsh Love Letter

Were all the peaks of Gwynedd
In one huge mountain piled,
Cnicht on Moelwyn,
Moel-y-gest, Moel Hebog,
And Eryri on top,
And all between us,
I'd climb them climb them
All!
To reach you.
O, how I love you!

Were all the streams of Gwynedd
In one great river joined,
Dwyfor, Dwyryd,
Glaslyn, Ogwen,
And Mawddach in flood,
And all between us,
I'd swim them swim them
All!
To reach you
O, how I love you!

Were all the forts of Gwynedd
In one great fortress linked,
Caer and castle,
Criccieth, Harlech,
Conwy, Caernarfon,
And all in flames,
I'd jump them jump them
All!
To reach you.
O, how I love you!

See you Saturday,
If it's not raining.

Michael Burn

from: *Ash on a Young Man's Sleeve*

We continued through the fairy-tale fields up to our ankles in grey mist and I gave my school scarf to Lydia to keep away the cold. She looked lovely in my green and gold scarf. I hummed the school song to myself:

> Green and Gold, Green and Gold,
> Strong be our hearts and bold.
> To remain unsullied our Great Name
> Adding to Ancient Glory, Modern Fame.
> Green and Gold, Green and...

I nearly stepped on some cow-dung, humming. At the top we gazed down at Cardiff, at the lights dotting the shadows below, window lights, lamp-posts, flashes of electricity from the trams. Away towards the direction of Newport a train rushed through the dark, a chain of lights, like a glimmering thought, across the blank mind of the countryside. Somewhere down there amongst the lights, Mother would be in the kitchen preparing the evening meal. Leo would be in his room writing a speech for some Labour Party meeting, rehearsing it perhaps before the mirror. Dad would be in the armchair under lamplight reading the *South Wales Echo*, the spectacles slipping down his nose, and his mouth silently forming the words as he read.

'I think Keith is very nice,' Lydia said.

'Yes, he's a good chap,' I condescended.

'And attractive too.' I looked at her – was she joking? 'Do you think so?' I asked doubtfully. I tried to see Keith through the eyes of Lydia. A scruffy, scraggy youth with red-brown hair falling over a high forehead without fuss – the freckled wide flat face, the snub nose, and eyes blue as a poison bottle...

'Oh, I don't mean physically,' said Lydia.

'No?'

'But he attracts me mentally.'

'That so?'

I was taken aback. Imagine *anybody* being attracted to Keith *mentally*. Perhaps Lydia was a little backward after all! But Lydia slipped her hand into mine.

'Of course *you* attract me mentally *and* physically,' she reassured me.

'I don't know why,' I said, 'there's nothing to me.' I looked at her beautiful face. 'Nothing at all really.'

'Oh, but there is,' protested Lydia.

'Besides, I'm no good for women,' I pointed out. 'I'm so selfish, so egocentric, inconsiderate. And I'm moody, shockingly moody. I think of suicide quite a lot, you know. I'd be hopeless to live with. Can't do anything in the house. Only concerned about myself. Yes, I'm an evil influence on women.'

'You shouldn't speak of yourself that way,' said Lydia passionately, 'You're a good person.'

'Oh no,' I protested. 'I'm rotten really, I know myself. Rotten through and through.'

The fields traced our signatures in moonlight and shadows. Under the clear stars we looked at each other with wonder, anew.

'You're beautiful in this light,' I said.

Lydia looked down at her feet.

'I'm going to kiss you,' I said.

She feebly tried to stop me. After she said: 'You're not like other boys. You kiss differently. You don't make me feel sick when you kiss me.' I wondered how other boys kissed her and *which* boys.

'How do you mean?' I questioned her.

'You keep your lips closed when you kiss,' she whispered. What did she mean? Of course I kept my lips closed. Was there another way of kissing?

I tried to embrace her again but she pushed me away saying:

'A girl mustn't be cheap with her kisses.'

We turned back down the path and later I stepped on the cowdung which earlier I had avoided.

Dannie Abse

from: *The Alone to the Alone*

In the Terraces, we never opposed love. The way we viewed this question was that love must be pretty deeply rooted to have gone on for so long. One would have to be very deep to tinker with so deep a root, deeper than we were. Also, love passes on the time. That is a prime feature in any place where there is a scarcity of work for the local men and women to do, a state which prevailed on a high plane indeed during the dark years now being spoken of. Also, love, properly used, keeps people warm. That is a fact of some importance when coal has to be considered as part of the groceries. Also, love possessing the power of making its subjects see things in a clearer light, creates a desire for beauty. This was interesting to us because if there was one thing the Terraces lacked more than any other it was that very beauty.

Our group which met nightly on the wall at the bottom of our backyard was agreed that never had so little beauty been compressed into so large a space as we saw in the Terraces. It was a clumsy bit of packing altogether. We took this in our solemn way to mean that when men consent to endure for too long the sadness of poverty and decline, beauty sees no point in staying, bows its head and goes. There was much poverty in the Terraces, nearly as much as air, weather or life. It achieved a variety of flavours and shapes that did credit to our originality and patience. Beneath its layers beauty lay in a mess and, no doubt, very dead. Men like artists who gallop after beauty should make a new set of divining rods, find out where hell is and put poverty in. Then beauty, rising like a rainbow from man's new dreams, would be pervasive as the mist of pettiness among us now and would come galloping after them for a change.

Among us, in the Terraces, love sometimes broke out. Love, making people see things in a clearer light, had a depressing effect. The Terraces, seen in a dim light that softened the curves, could give a man a bellyache that nothing short of a hot water bottle atop the belly could ease. Therefore, to see the Terraces in any hard, revelatory light such as would be given off by a kerosene flare or passion, would make the lover wish for the very opposite of the Terraces. That opposite would be beauty. So beneath the dark waters of the stream along whose banks we lived, pinched, scraped and pondered, there would sometimes flash the forms of beauty desired and we got much joy from watching these flashing, brief, uncatchable forms. They were the promise of life in a community that had come as near to a general stoppage of living as any community can come without staging a mass execution.

'But the most important thing about love, though,' said my friend Walter, 'is that it keeps people warm. That's more important even than love considered as a means to breeding to a man who hasn't got the means to go filling his outhouse with coal. To that man, anything that puts him in a position not to care about the state of his outhouse is a very big thing. That's a bigger thing even than man's having been descended from the apes.'

And, with the exception of my friend Ben, who had seen a chimpanzee in Bostock's menagerie and who thought that it was a very great achievement to have worked one's way up from being just an ape, we were all pretty much of this love-is-warmth school of thought for which my friend Walter always took up the tongs. We thought this the more interesting because we ourselves were too old, plain or politically conscious to be in the running for any love that might be knocking about. My friend Walter was a very cold subject except about the brain where he always had a spout of deep ideas that kept his skull warm. My friend Ben was married. My friend Arthur has some stomach trouble that seemed to him to be a fair summing up of all that was wrong with the world, and the viewpoint of my friend Arthur was pretty dark on most topics. There was nothing particularly wrong with me. My stomach was in order. I was single. But women, to me, never seemed to be more than just me all over again. A bit quicker to become mothers, I being a man, and a bit slower to use the vote, but with no more difference than that. We shared the floor space of a zoo and kept the place as tidy as we could during our journey through it. I could never look upon women with the zeal that came so easily to the bulk of my fellow-voters.

This did not prevent us from taking a keen interest in those of our neighbours who were visited by love. Sometimes, the love worked out all wrongly and made a mess of these neighbours, such a mess as caused my friend Walter to say that if men wanted to weep as much as they had good reason to, they would have to carry a ten-gallon reserve tear tank strapped to their back to be brought into play for special sessions of this weeping business. Sometimes it would make these neighbours slightly dafter than they had been, and this meant that we would be a bit busier than ever going around explaining to these neighbours whose minds had been laid waste in patches by passion, such facts as the rising cost of living and the weaknesses of a competitive society which we thought should rank as high in the consideration of these neighbours as the itch for union of bodies in love. Or, love would leave them as it found them, which did not say much for them or for the brand of love they went in for. Or it would set them alight and the warmth from their burning would be very pleasant to such sad and continually frozen types as ourselves.

Gwyn Thomas

Letter from John

It was not for want of think
that I did not rite you a love letter sooner
and this cause I think of you every hour of the day
and every day of the year
and I do love your father to cause he did lend you the horse
and cart to brought me to the train on Monday.
I shall never forget to remember what you did tell
me when coming in the cart. Oh! Mary Jane
stick to your promise won't you my dear.

I did rive Pontyprydd safe and sound
and I did go strait to the Shop
and when the master did see me he did say

'Man from where are you?'
And I told him that I was John from Maenclochog
coming to work in his shop. Then he nowed me in a minit.

Look you my work is selling cotten
and tapes and hundreds of other things.
They do call it Happy Compartment
or something, but indeed to goodness
it was not very happy at all to be here without you,
the girl I do love better than nobody
(for all the time I am thinking of you)

Oh, yes you will ask my mother to send my watch
if it is working
cause it will be very handy for me in the morning
to know what o'clock it is.
She do know my directions.

There is a lot of girls in this shop
but not one to match you Mary Jane.
How long you are going to stop
in Mrs. Jones' again, Mary Jane,
cause I will try and get you a job at Pontyprydd
to be a Millander.
I will hask Mr. Thomas the draper about a position for you
for they say he do give very good vittels to his clerks.
It will be better by half for you to come
to Pontyprydd cause then we will be near to one another
for the forehead of Mrs. Thomas' shop
and the forehead of our shop
be quite close to one another
and by and by we will marry
is it not my dear?

They say that shop girls do not make good wifes
but you know what Mr. Evans the schoolmaster said:
'Put a nose wherever you like
and it will be a nose

and put a donkey wherever you like
and it will be a donkey.'
And like that you are Mary my dear.
I believe shop girls will make good wifes
if they have a chance.

Well, I will not rite you a bigger this time
for if it was twice bigger I could never
tell you how I love you.

I send you a piece of Poultry
I did make last night
and if you have not received it
send back at once.

I must finish cause I can hear somebody
asking for hooks and eyes
and your loving John must go forward.

*

Oh Mary Jane my darling
I love you in my heart
I told you so last monday
When coming in the cart

Suppose the horse did understand
What I to you did say
I have no doubt my darling
It would have runned away.

I'll always love you Mary Jane
And you be true to me
Come up soon to Pontyprydd
to sell some Drapery.

Tony Curtis

(A found poem, from a letter dated 1908, discovered
among my grandmother's possessions after her death.)

24

A Letter

Alun Lewis to Freda Aykroyd, 1943

Oh such wealth, great caskets of sunlight unlocked pouring
all over me like the water in the lake – *all* your letters – three
envelopes of your letters – all waiting here today... There isn't
anything I can do with this fullness except feel and bless it –
do I need to *convey* it to you, darling?... There are situations,
obligations, yes, yes, yes – but not now: nor when we meet
again... I dream of this other time, of deep freedom – ...
I do grieve, I know that. I don't let myself hate because hate
spoils – it withers & shrinks like socks in salt water, but grief
pours gentleness liquidly round everything and it's a natural
expression for the love & the melancholy that almost, I think,
I like best... Don't worry about my love, will you, or your own
love? Hands are safe, are gentle, are kind.

from: *Gwalchmai's Boast*

It is splendid I am, fearless in battle.
Before the host I'm a lion, like lightning my onset.
Guarding the borders I've watched this night out.
Murmuring fords, water of Dygen Freiddin,
Bright green the virgin grass, lovely the water,
Loud the nightingale's familiar song.
The seagulls sport on the bed of the flood,
Their plumage gleams, their factions are turbulent.
Because I love a young girl of Caerwys
In early summer my memory wanders...
I've listened to lips in true contentment
And the gentle sounding speech of a girl.
But for noble Owain's sake, fetter of foes,
The English scatter before my blade.

Gwalchmai ap Meilyr (1130-1180)
(tr. Tony Conran)

My Courtship of Miss Roberts

We sat in the garden at Penylan
with jugs of squash, walnut cake,
and flights of wasps landing on the jam.
Her mother would look through a porthole
to observe my dance,
the ritual steps of courtship
as it used to be done –
cock and hen in gentility's trance.

Miss Roberts wore pastel shifts
and a medallion for the Barry swim.
She liked to quote Rubert Brooke
and like Ava Gardner
had a cleft in her chin.
We would sit very quiet until the orange sun sank
and mother brought out the tea.
Cucumber triangles and peace
and responsibility smiling at me.

John Tripp

Englyn

My warm breast I give you, sweet wretch,
My life if you wish it.
My hand in your hand
All my strength with it.

Anon., 17th century
(tr. Siân James)

from: *Dragons & Roses*

'God Hywel, I've got to make a phone call,' said Rhiannon, 'I forgot to let the vicar know that the dress rehearsal isn't till Thursday. Come with me to the kiosk, love — I haven't got my glasses. Gareth, get Barbara a drink will you, love. We won't be five minutes.'

Almost before I'd realised what was happening, they'd gone out together.

'I don't want another drink,' I told Gareth. 'Honestly, I've still got this one.'

'You may as well,' he said. 'Come on. They'll be gone quite a time.'

He turned his doleful, animal-brown eyes towards me with what seemed a significant glance.

'You don't mean... You can't mean that she's just... well, taken him off to...'

'Yes,' he said. 'There's a phone over there, look, if she'd wanted to phone. She'll see the vicar in church tomorrow.'

'Well then, let's go after them,' I said, getting to my feet. 'We'll say we didn't want another drink. Let's go after them.'

'She's got the car, though, hasn't she? They're on the other side of town by this time. Don't be upset. We can enjoy ourselves without them, can't we?'

'But Hywel's my husband,' I said.

'Oh Christ, I didn't know that. I didn't know he was married. I hadn't heard that. I'm very sorry. I wouldn't have said anything if I'd known you two were married. Not for the world.'

'I'd have guessed, I suppose,' I said miserably.

'They'll be quite a time, half an hour at least. Perhaps only talking. She and Hywel – I think they talk more than anything else. They talk and cry over each other. Rhiannon pretends to be empty-headed, but she can be very serious and emotional at times. Let's have another drink.'

'I don't drink, Gareth, honestly. I've had too much already.'

I had. To my embarrassment my eyes had filled with tears and one or two were already running down my face.

He drew his chair nearer to me. 'Don't worry about Rhiannon,' he said. 'God, she's only having pre-wedding nerves and wanting attention. She doesn't mean any harm by it.'

'Yes she does,' I said. 'She seems determined to harm me.'

'No, it's not intentional. Listen, Barbara, you don't exist for Rhiannon. Honestly.'

'Is that supposed to comfort me?'

'I could comfort you,' he said. 'Oh, I don't mean anything wrong. I only mean we could go out into the garden and have a bit of a talk out there while we're waiting for them to come back. We could stand by the wall where nobody could see us and then they'd have to worry about us, wouldn't they? They'd have to look for us. That is, if you really don't want another drink.'

It seemed a good idea. Better, anyway, than counting the minutes till they returned, wondering what they were doing. Anything was better than that.

'All right,' I said. Why shouldn't Hywel wonder where I was. Why shouldn't he worry about me. Let him worry.

I followed Gareth out of the bar along a dark passage which led to the garden. It was already half-dark.

There were geraniums along the low wall fronting the road. I remember the acrid smell of the geraniums, the smell of the beer from the open window behind us, the sour taste of gin in my mouth. Bitterness. Let him worry. God, I hoped he'd worry.

We went to the far side of the garden, to a dark corner between a high wall and some out-houses, and without further word Gareth pulled me towards him and started to kiss me.

I suppose it was what I had expected. I certainly wasn't offended or hurt or anything like that.

'Now, don't cry any more,' he was saying in between kissing me. 'Pretty girls like you shouldn't cry.'

He was very tall, his body was soft, not exactly fat but not hard and bony like Hywel's – more comforting, somehow, less masculine. His lips were very soft and gentle.

He really enjoyed kissing.

After a time he seemed to be taking gentle little bites at my lips. It was nice. I found my anger leaving me. After a while I did the same to him.

'Waiting is all right, isn't it?' he said. 'You see, you feel better now. I knew you would.'

'It's better than making conversation in pubs anyway,' I said.

'You shouldn't bother,' he said. 'You can get by without conversation. I do.'

He found my mouth again. To Gareth, kissing seemed an end in itself. He devoted himself to it as though he had nothing else to attend to, as though there was nothing else in the world. Hywel was always too impatient to kiss properly.

We kissed until the dark fell round us, until there wasn't a glimpse of light in the sky, till I hardly knew where I was.

When we separated at last and reached for breath, I found, without too much surprise, that he had opened my blouse and was trying to undo my bra.

'Let me do it,' I said. 'It's a terrible clasp.'

He held my breasts in his hands with great care, as though he was guessing· their weight. 'Oh, you are a lovely girl,' he said.

'I don't think I want to...you know. Well, I don't think I ought to anyway.'

'Oh no, nothing like that. I said I didn't mean anything wrong. Definitely not.'

He took my breasts in his mouth, first one and then the other.

It was lovely, full of gentleness and homage, it seemed: lovely. Unfortunately it began to excite me.

'No more,' I said, pushing his head away.

'Oh, there's no harm at all in this,' he said. 'Oh, I did this as a baby.' He sounded so earnest that I couldn't help smiling. He started licking my nipples, pressing both together, licking both together. His face was dark against my whiteness.

'That's enough,' I said sharply.

He stood up, then, gazing down at my breasts and sighing. 'Put them back, then,' he said, as though they were pets, rabbits or something, I'd had out for an airing.

'You're very nice,' I said.

'And you're so generous with your lovely things. Some women are so hostile and mean.'

'I bet you usually get what you want,' I said. 'You get what you want by being so kind and gentle. If I had more time, and if I'd had time to think about it beforehand, I'd want to... you know... and I would too...I think I would.'

'I'd want to as well, I can tell you that. We could give each other such a lot. We're both generous, you see. We're both givers – not like Hywel and Rhiannon. God, those two would bankrupt anyone.'

We kissed again, as gently and tenderly as before. He nuzzled my ear like a pony.

Then, before taking me back into the pub, he combed my hair. Even that he turned into a pleasurable and sensuous experience, taking his time over it, turning it this way and that, pressing it to his face, exclaiming over its length and thickness. A last kiss, very long and soft. 'Now, we're not miserable any more, are we? We're all right – kissed all better.'

We were sitting on the same chairs at the same table when Rhiannon and Hywel came back.

'Sorry we were so long,' Rhiannon said in her most musical tones as she pushed through the tables towards us.

'What the hell kept you?' Gareth asked, but in a slow, lazy voice, as though he didn't really care.

'We couldn't get through,' she said. 'We were about fifteen minutes getting through.'

'And then we talked outside for a while,' Hywel said, as though concerned to present a more plausible case.

'I'd better run you two home now, I suppose. Do you want to come, Gareth?'

'No,' he said. 'I'll stay here.'

He didn't get to his feet or smile at her as she got up to go.

I pressed against him as I followed her and Hywel out to the car. And very gently, he ran his hand up my leg.

Siân James

Marlene

When I first kissed you
up against a wall
in Westbury Street
you had a woolly pully on
I had a hard.
Lip smacked lip
tongue sucked tongue
and never said a word.
A cat miaowed.
A light went out –
and nothing else stirred:
there was no-one around
there was nothing behind
the blinds in Westbury Street
nor all the Universe
but you and I
like little limpets
struggling for breath

Alan Perry

Englyn to the Penis

A puking merry prick is this, a nice burden
in maidens' crotches;
a holy-water sprinkler spitting soap,
arse beater, God's grace on it.

Anon., late 16th century
(tr. Dafydd Johnston)

from: *Shifts*

In the couple of weeks he'd been working, Mrs Williams, the landlady had changed remarkably.

Not that she was a real landlady like the Blackpool postcards. In fact, she wasn't bad for her age, which must have been the early forties. She wore rollers to excess and clasped her wrists in the appropriate Mona Lisa way while talking, but still, she was all right. He suspected that probably most roller wearing wrist claspers were really averagely human.

She was a widow, and worked in a factory from eight to half past four. The factory made electrical components, she told him, but she didn't know what they were for.

At first she had shown a kind of reserved sympathy for Jack's being unemployed but this had worn away to lack of faith as he failed to get a job. This turned to something like friendship when he got work and started setting the alarm clock. But he'd changed his attitude to her too. It was 'Connie' and 'John' now. And that uncertainty you get between owner and tenant when neither is quite sure how to play the part. No meter in the bathroom, an amateur fumbling of the money when it fell due on Fridays.

She ought to call him Jack. It was only because of seeing his signature she called him John. His father had called him John and then Jack had read somewhere Jack was short for John and had adopted it. His mother had called him Shwn or Shwna after the local fashion, or rather old fashion, which at least was better than John, but as a kid he'd liked Jack best of all. She should call him it. After all, he called her Connie, which was short for something. Constance probably. The virtue of being stable and reliable. 'Call me Jack. Everybody does.' He practised saying it. Slipping fully back into the patois it was 'everybody do' — except nobody do, or did when he should have said it, because then he hadn't known anybody, having no job.

He was not yet, after all, back in his home town. After nearly two hundred miles, he had stopped exactly two val-leys short. Over the mountain to the west of his digs was the steelworks, over the mountain to the west of that, home. The end of the salmon ladder, where the bog door had no bolt. Except there was no bog door that was his there now, and hence.

But still, even here things had a familiarity he was constantly catching out of the corner of his eye. The moor between Accrington and Blackburn, he'd thought, had been close, and the colour of the light on a trip to Howarth with Liz had almost rung home bells, but here there was. He wasn't sure what it was. Places remembered from childhood. Dead, grassed tips that only a practised eye could spot. And the true clichés: sheep that vandalized housing estates, shitten ponies gone feral, men like Ben sitting around the bilingual war memorial wearing their flat caps when the weather picked up. And something else. Or nothing. Landlady stories. It's about the ceiling Mrs W. Yes Mr P? Well I'd like to have one. Don't worry, the neighbours don't walk around much. And while I'm at it Mrs W, can I wheel my bike up your back passage? No, put it in the front between the railings. You know Mrs W, they don't bury people here; they sit them in The Prince of Wales lounge bar with a pint of Albright. Local councillors are going to take measures. Two gills of vodka and a litre of scotch. Et cetera. And then there were the familiar names on the destination boards of buses. That was part of the something. Once, a busdriver he'd recognised, the father of a former friend. A man who'd known his father, worked with him, years and years ago. Before he was born. The busdriver hadn't recognised him. Jack did not let on. He could have done. Hello, Mr Watkins. I'm Jack. I was at school with your son, Keith. Remember? All that excavating. No.

What would she say if he said it this Friday?

There we are, Connie. Eleven pound. Thank you John love. Oh, call me Jack. Everybody do. Oh right. Jack.

They were both too amateur though. She might think, after all this time, it was an opening move. He would surely have said it sooner if it was innocent.

She was still attractive. And the house ached with the gap left by her husband. There was one photograph, black and white, that froze the unnatural wedding moment, the husband looking as if he'd be happier in winklepickers and a shoelace tie, she looking older than him with a horsetoothed, forced smile. Just that on the stereogram that probably dated from one of their early Christmases. Although the house was well furnished, the central heating adequate, corners of rooms seemed remote and cold. Just too big, he supposed. One of those big terraced houses with a bay window and a stained glass Viking ship in the front door, like the house where an uncle and auntie probably still lived, two valleys away.

Perhaps they would exchange looks. A coy come-on. All right, Jack then, she would say. He would go to the rugby club with her and be shy and young while she introduced him to her friends. The openhearted would say good luck to them. The grown-up daughter living in Newport would find out and be upset, confused. Why, Mam? This isn't like you. Connie would blossom, look younger. If we could give each other a few years. He would shave more often. She would exorcise her husband's ghost and, flouting convention, they'd be perfectly happy. Jack, it's been so long, she'd say when they did it, gently, in the early morning. *The Indian Summer of Mrs Williams.* Fade in violins. Roll credits.

Christopher Meredith

The Shirt of a Lad

As I did the washing one day
  Under the bridge at Aberteifi,
  And a golden stick to drub it,
  And my sweetheart's shirt beneath it –
  A knight came by upon a charger,
  Proud and swift and broad of shoulder,
  And he asked if I would sell
  The shirt of the lad that I loved well.

No, I said, I will not trade –
  Not if a hundred pounds were paid;
  Not if two hillsides I could keep
  Full with wethers and white sheep;

Not if two fields full of oxen
Under yoke were in the bargain;
Not if the herbs of all Llanddewi
Trodden and pressed, were offered to me –
Not for the likes of that, I'd sell
The shirt of the lad that I love well.

Anon., 16th century
(tr. Tony Conran)

To a Nun

Please God, forsake your water and dry bread
And fling the bitter cress you eat aside.
Put by your rosary. In Mary's name
Leave chanting creeds to mildewing monks in Rome.
Spring is at work in woodlands bright with sun;
Springtime's not made for living like a nun.
Your faith, my fairest lady, your religion
Show but a single face of love's medallion.
Slip on this ring and this green gown, these laces;
The wood is furnitured with resting-places.
Hide in the birch-tree's shade – upon your knees
Murmur the mass of cuckoos, litanies
Of spring's green foliage. There's no sacrilege
If we find heaven here against the hedge.
Remember Ovid's book and Ovid's truth:
There's such a thing as having too much faith.
Let us discover the shapes, the earthly signs
Of our true selves, our souls, among the vines.
For surely God and all his saints above,
High in their other heaven, pardon love.

John Ormond
(after the 15th century Welsh)

35

from: *The Minister*

I know the place, under the hedge
In the top meadow; it was where my mam
Got into trouble, and only the stars
Were witness of the secret act.
They say her mother was the same.
Well, why not? It's hard on a girl
In these old hills, where youth is short
And boys are scarce; and the ones we'd marry
Are poor or shy. But Job's got money,
And his wife is old. Don't look at me
Like that, Job; I'm trying to listen
To what the minister says. Your eyes
Scare me, yet my bowels ache
With a strange frenzy. This is what
My mother and her mother felt
For the men who took them under the hedge.

R.S. Thomas

from: *The Saviour*

Inside the house the yellowish heat of the room was oppressive and motionless. A scalding yellow shawl drawn like a curtain across the window dimmed the air and tried to withhold the strong sunlight from the red hump of fire smouldering in the grate. Flies laboured in a ring before an indistinguishable picture hung above the tarred chimneypiece. After the uproar of the hammering upon the door the grey girl rocked herself from side to side, dim and unreal as a phantom in the shadows of a settle, babbling to herself and fretfully boring with her large fingers into the palms of her hands. She was a tall grey-clad figure, very angular and a hunchback, dressed in clothes similar to her mother's but the shapeless and baggy garments were pale grey, the heavy skirt and the thick fringed shawl folded around her humped shoulders were of silvery greyish wool. She wore a sort of soiled handkerchief spread out on top of the plentiful and fluffy hair of her head. Her small bony face was thin and underdeveloped and, apart from her eyes, large, abject and gentle, she was hideous. A sickly greyish skin moist with grease covered her watchful sharp-edged features, and a pair of taut sinews strained in unrelaxed and ugly prominence across her sunken cheeks. But, as she sat with the yellow gloom falling upon her glistening skin and her pallid clothes, she looked dim and unsubstantial, her pale face and her uncoloured fluffy hair and the nacrous bulges of her red-rimmed eyes made her appear spectral and shadowy, her figure seemed almost transparent in its greyish coverings. In the stupefying heat she no longer prayed but jabbered on about the trees and the primroses and the buds.

Spring had come once, daily her uneasy heart had watched it through its bars. Morning after morning she had heard the throaty lecherous whistle of the thrush, and looking out into a raw dawn she saw the sky glow dull and red as the back of a mirror. She went down into the misty field when the vast shadows lying upon the earth were still white with hoarfrost and sat crouching in the hedge, fearing the long flock of starlings that wavered low overhead like the skin of a spotted serpent. She gazed with her bulging whitish eyes at the small dewdrops on the faces of the pale primroses, the minute drops of moisture like a tiny perspiration spread out upon the yellow petals, and when the curve of birds writhed by again she hurried home fearfully, high shouldered and with long strides. Each morning she escaped to the field and at last the buds of the little horse-chestnut in the hedge began to crack open upon their branches. She stood gazing in ecstasy at the fine white velvet of the breaking buds, the delicate grey-green birth-fur covering the infant leaves as they unfolded from their husky glues. She stood forgetful, watching the static gesticulation of those little grey-gloved hands, the grey-green herringbone of the leaves standing up crumpled from the splitting buds.

And then suddenly she heard a shout. She looked round, it was the radiance of broad daylight and the great trees were drying in the sun. Her heart seemed to leave her body and return again burning like a hot spark to her breast. Up the gritty path she ran, avoiding the demented old woman who waited massive and wine-faced with fury at the roadside, striking a convulsive blow at her with her red stick as she passed. She reached the house and flinging herself with prayers into the kitchen settle, waited in agony to see the loutish figure fill the door.

Glyn Jones

from: *Blind Date*

I said, 'What about turning back?'

'Turning back? No fear. Afraid or something?'

It's easy for her to talk: she knows this Frank boy. Been with him before. But not one of us has ever seen Henri, though she seems to think he's a farm-hand.

A farm-hand! My dreams don't include farm-hands. My dreams turn round students. Tall handsome students with long scarves around their necks. Students with piles of books under their arms. Merry, noisy students like those I see from the bus at Bangor. Nice respectable students – ministerials like the ones who come for a walk with us to Llyn Rhos Ddu before evening service. Like Mr Harrington.

'How old is this Henri?' I asked as we neared Fern Hill.

'Same age as Frank, I suppose.'

'How old is Frank?'

'Twenty-one.'

'Twenty-one?' Heavens above, that's old.'

'You've moaned enough about schoolboys being too young for you. Don't worry. Everything will be all right as long as you don't let Henri put his tongue in your mouth.'

'Put his tongue in my mouth? Ugh!'

'It's a boy's place to try, a girl's place to refuse him.'

'Does Frank try?'

'Every boy tries.'

'What did *you* do?'

'Tell him not to.'

'And he listened?' If anyone tried it on me he'd never see the colour of me again.

'Of course he did. Do you know Olwen? Do you know what Olwen did to a boy from Llangefni way last Saturday night?' She looks into the quick of my eyes and smiles. 'She bit off a piece of his tongue.'

'Bit it off?' I can't swallow because there's a lump like a potato in my throat.

'He had to go to hospital for four stitches.'

I feel quite ill, am cold all over from thinking what I'd do should this boy Henri try such nonsense. Henri's a silly name. An old-fashioned, ugly name. A name to put anybody to shame. How can anyone with a name like that be handsome?

'Why?' I asked coyly, 'Why do boys want to put their tongues in your mouth?'

'To make you sleep, of course.'

'Oh!'

'And while you're asleep they lift up your clothes, pull down your knickers, and give you a baby.'

I feel my legs giving under me. I feel my inside caving in. I was always a one for jibbing it.

Jane Edwards
(tr. D. Llwyd Morgan)

Bundling

I was beloved where I was one night,
the brevity of the night was a betrayal.
Oh Mary, I was sorry to see a skylark
and dawn yesterday and the light of day.
The day which belonged to two,
it caught us between my love's hands.
I don't know of any other couple in all the land
lying together so lovingly.
I didn't have her complaining stridently
although we got into the same bed.
Rarely do we fight,
and one cry will cause our deaths.
The cheeks do not hide a man's trouble,
for days I have been a troubled man.
It is grief in my face
grieving for her face.
It was poison for me from a gentle girl,
by securing a meeting it was medicine.
The slender maid's hands, love of a man,
knew well how to hold an outlaw.

We threw in short loops
four arms around four breasts.
My state pleased me greatly,
around my neck they yoked me.
Around my back to drive me out of my mind,
binding of a roebuck, so was I bound.
Was there ever a more agonising death
to take me from the world with my little darling?
My sweetheart is gentle in all conversation,
and ungentle as regards the bliss.
My breast is a saint,
and the enemies are the knees.

On my oath I am older
than the wolf by many a year.
Lying awake at night by the banks of the streams
without an hour's sleep brings on old age.
Hywel's manner, brilliant praise,
is not dissimilar to that of the owl:
staying awake from night to night,
hiding as the day comes;
silent skulking like a hermit
and dumb watching without getting
    anything more.
We lay naked side by side
suffering the same pain nightly
without intending, my slender darling,
sin anymore than little children.
I am having with her the colour of snow
a relationship like twins:
loving to walk and roam together,
I wouldn't love my sister any more;
loving amorous greeting and chat,
the love of innocent young children.
Great is the weak brigand's love,
greater is the sin of a little boy.

> *Hywel Dafi, 15th century*
> *(tr. Dafydd Johnston)*

from: *Extraordinary Little Cough*

Three girls, all fair, came down the cliff-side arm in arm, dressed in short, white trousers. Their arms and legs and throats were brown as berries; I could see when they laughed that their teeth were very white; they stepped on to the beach, and Brazell and Skully stopped singing. Sidney smoothed his hair back, rose casually, put his hands in his pockets, and walked towards the girls, who now stood close together, gold and brown, admiring the sunset with little attention, patting their scarves, turning smiles on each other. He stood in front of them, grinned, and saluted: 'Hallo, Gwyneth! Do you remember me?'

'La-di-da!' whispered Dan at my side, and made a mock salute to George still peering at the retreating sea.

'Well, if this isn't a surprise!' said the tallest girl. With little studi
ed movements of her hands, as though she were distributing flowers, she introduced Peggy and Jean.

Fat Peggy, I thought, too jolly for me, with hockey legs and tomboy crop, was the girl for Dan; Sidney's Gwyneth was a distinguished piece and quite sixteen, as immaculate and unapproachable as a girl in Ben Evans's stores; but Jean, shy and curly, with butter-coloured hair, was mine. Dan and I walked slowly to the girls.

I made up two remarks: 'Fair's fair, Sidney, no bigamy abroad,' and 'Sorry we couldn't arrange to have the sea in when you came.'

Jean smiled, wiggling her heel in the sand, and I raised my cap.

'Hallo!'

The cap dropped at her feet.

As I bent down, three lumps of sugar fell from my blazer pocket. 'I've been feeding a horse,' I said, and began to blush guiltily when all the girls laughed.

I could have swept the ground with my cap, kissed my hand gaily, called them señoritas, and made them smile without tolerance. Or I could have stayed at a distance, and this would have been better still, my hair blown in the wind, though there was no wind at all that evening, wrapped in mystery and staring at the sun, too aloof to speak to girls; but I knew that all the time my ears would have been burning, my stomach would have been as hollow and as full of voices as a shell. 'Speak to them quickly, before they go away!' a voice would have said insistently over the dramatic silence, as I stood like Valentino on the edge of the bright, invisible bull-ring of the sands. 'Isn't it lovely here!' I said.

I spoke to Jean alone; and this is love, I thought, as she nodded her head and swung her curls and said: 'It's nicer than Porthcawl.'

Brazell and Skully were two big bullies in a nightmare; I forgot them when Jean and I walked up the cliff, and, looking back to see if they were baiting George again or wrestling together, I saw that George had disappeared around the corner of the rocks and that they were talking at the foot of the cliff with Sidney and the two girls.

'What's your name?'

I told her.

'That's Welsh,' she said.

'You've got a beautiful name.'

'Oh! it's just ordinary.'

'Shall I see you again?'

'If you want to.'

'I want to all right! We can go and bathe in the morning. And we can try to get an eagle's egg. Did you know that there were eagles here?'

'No,' she said. 'Who was that handsome boy on the beach, the tall one with dirty trousers?'

'He's not handsome, that's Brazell. He never washes or combs his hair or anything. He's a bully and he cheats.'

'I think he's handsome.'

We walked into Button's field, and I showed her inside the tents and gave her one of George's apples. 'I'd like a cigarette,' she said.

It was nearly dark when the others came. Brazell and Skully were with Gwyneth, one on each side of her holding her arms, Sidney was with Peggy, and Dan walked, whistling, behind with his hands in his pockets.

'There's a pair,' said Brazell, 'they've been here all alone and they aren't even holding hands. You want a pill,' he said to me.

'Build Britain's babies,' said Skully.

'Go on!' Gwyneth said. She pushed him away from her but she was laughing, and she said nothing when he put his arm around her waist.

'What about a bit of fire?' said Brazell.

Jean clapped her hands like an actress. Although I knew I loved her, I didn't like anything she said or did.

'Who's going to make it?'

'He's the best, I'm sure,' she said, pointing to me.

Dan and I collected sticks, and by the time it was quite dark there was a fire crackling. Inside the sleeping-tent, Brazell and Jean sat close together; her golden head was on his shoulder; Skully, near them, whispered to Gwyneth; Sidney unhappily held Peggy's hand.

'Did you every see such a sloppy lot?' I said, watching Jean smile in the fiery dark.

'Kiss me, Charley!' said Dan.

We sat by the fire in the corner of the field. The sea, far out, was still making a noise. We heard a few nightbirds. '"Tu-whit! tu-whoo!" Listen! I don't like owls,' Dan said, 'they scratch your eyes out!' – and tried not to listen to the soft voices in the tent. Gwyneth's laughter floated out over the suddenly moonlit field, but Jean, with the beast, was smiling and silent in the covered warmth; I knew her little hand was in Brazell's hand.

'Women!' I said.

Dylan Thomas

A Term of Pan

Even the gilt frame holds a dark
Muscular life, retains its
Dirty gold longer than the skin.

These bodies stretching through
A sensual world might be laughable,
A shamed ideal, and yet the hard

Triumphant flesh remains as
Innocent as paint. The limbs of girls
Divide and coil like flames, the men's

Goathair hangs sleek as wet seaweed,
As in this blue ridiculous grove
The rite of skin on skin, skin on earth

Is suspended for the moment of eternity,
While lovers douse their whiteness in shadow,
Wait endlessly for what flesh promises.

Robert Minhinnick

Traditional Verse

The tender harp with sweetness laden
Is like a tender sweet-fleshed maiden.
In seclusion gently touch her,
She will prove the sweeter, sweeter

Anon., 16th-17th century
(tr. Siân James)

from: *One Warm Saturday*

'There never was a young lover who didn't love the moon.' Mr O'Brien gave the young man a cheery smile, and patted his hand. His own hand was red and hairy. 'I could see at the flash of a glance that Lou and this nice young fellow were made for each other. I could see it in their eyes. Dear me, no! I'm not so old and blind I can't see love in front of my nose. Couldn't you see it, Marjorie?'

In the long silence, Lou collected glasses from the cupboard as though she had not heard Mr O'Brien speak. She drew the curtains, shut out the moon, sat on the edge of her bed with her feet tucked under her, looked at her photograph as at a stranger, folded her hands as she folded them, on the first meeting, before the young man's worship in the Gardens.

'A host of angels must be passing by,' said Mr O'Brien. 'What a silence there is! Have I said anything out of place? Drink and be merry, to-morrow we die. What do you think I bought these lovely shining botttles for?'

The bottles were opened. The dead were lined on the mantelpiece. The whisky went down. Harold the barman and Marjorie, her dress lifted, sat in the one arm-chair together. Mrs Franklin, with Ernie's head on her lap, sang in a sweet, trained contralto voice *The Shepherd's Lass*. Mr O'Brien kept rhythm with his foot.

I want Lou in my arms, the young man said to himself, watching Mr O'Brien tap and smile and the barman draw Marjorie down deep. Mrs Franklin's voice sang sweetly in the small bedroom where he and Lou should be lying in the white bed without any smiling company to see them drown. He and Lou could go down together, one cool body weighted with a boiling stone, on to the falling, blank white, entirely empty sea, and never rise. Sitting on their bridal bed, near enough to hear his breath, she was farther from him than before they met. Then he had everything but her body; now she had given him two kisses, and everything had vanished but that beginning. He must be good and patient with Mr O'Brien. He could wipe away the embracing, old smile with the iron back of his hand. Sink lower, lower, Harold and Marjorie, tumble like whales at Mr O'Brien's feet.

He wished that the light would fail. In the darkness he and Lou could creep beneath the clothes and imitate the dead. Who would look for them there, if they were dead still and soundless? The others would shout to them down the dizzy stairs or rummage in the silence about the narrow, obstacled corridors or stumble out into the night to search for them among the cranes and ladders in the desolation of the destroyed houses. He could hear, in the made-up dark, Mr O'Brien's voice cry, 'Lou, where are you? Answer! answer!' the hollow answer of the echo, 'answer!' and hear her lips in the cool pit of the bed secretly move around another name and feel them move.

Dylan Thomas

Lovers

The two men in the road were taken aback
The lovers came out shading their eyes from the sun,
And never was white so white, or black so black,
As her cheeks and hair. 'There are more things than one
A man might turn into a wood for, Jack,'
Said George; Jack whispered: 'He has not got a gun.
It's a bit too much of a good thing, I say.
They are going the other road, look. And see her run.'–
She ran. 'What a thing it is, this picking may!'

Edward Thomas

from: *Under Milk Wood*

Mog Edwards and Miss Price

First Voice

From where you are you can hear in Cockle Row in the spring, moonless night, Miss Price, dressmaker and sweet-shop-keeper, dream of

Second Voice

her lover, tall as the town clock tower, Samson-syrup-gold-maned, whacking thighed and piping hot, thunderbolt-bass'd and barnacle-breasted, flailing up the cockles with his eyes like blowlamps and scooping low over her lonely loving hot-waterbottled body.

Mr Edwards

Myfanwy Price!

Miss Price

Mr Mog Edwards!

Mr Edwards

I am a draper mad with love. I love you more than all the flannelette and calico, candlewick, dimity, crash and merino, tussore, cretonne, crepon, muslin, poplin, ticking and twill in the whole Cloth Hall of the world. I have come to take you away to my Emporium on the hill, where the change hums on wires. Throw away your little bedsocks and your Welsh wool knitted jacket, I will warm the sheets like an electric toaster, I will lie by your side like the Sunday roast.

Miss Price

I will knit you a wallet of forget-me-not blue, for the money to be comfy. I will warm your heart by the fire so that you can slip it in under your vest when the shop is closed.

Mr Edwards

Myfanwy, Myfanwy, before the mice gnaw at your bottom drawer will you say

Miss Price

Yes, Mog, yes, Mog, yes, yes, yes.

Mr Edwards

And all the bells of the tills of the town shall ring for our wedding.

Dylan Thomas

Spring Wedding

Suddenly, from a winter of committees,
bitter funerals, in spring sunshine
this: the flowers, dresses,

sly and bawdy sillinesses as big-
breasted bridesmaids pose on the
grass all nerves and perfume.

Embarrassed in borrowed fur, the
mother, tripping up to laughs, feigns
coyness at the verger's flirt.

And with her starched and baffled father
comes the bride, as all brides lovely,
calm for the boy who is Man

at sight of her and vaults his vows,
loud, excited, rams
home the ring and weeps
daft tears on the registers.

And I would with him, this honourable
Spring, anticipating nothing.

Philip Owens

from: *The Mabinogion*

Pwyll, prince of Dyfed, was at Arberth, a chief court of his, with a feast prepared for him, and great hosts of men along with him. And after the first sitting Pwyll arose to take a walk, and made for the top of a mound which was above the court and was called Gorsedd Arberth. 'Lord,' said one of the court, 'it is the peculiarity of the mound that whatever high-born man sits upon it will not go thence without one of two things: wounds or blows, or else his seeing a wonder.' 'I do not fear to receive wounds or blows amidst such a host as this, but as to the wonder, I should be glad to see that. I will go,' said he, 'to the mound, to sit'.

He sat upon the mound. And as they were sitting down, they could see a lady on a big fine pale white horse, with a garment of shining gold brocaded silk upon her, coming along the highway that led past the mound. The horse had a slow even pace, as he thought who saw it, and was coming level with the mound. 'Men,' said Pwyll, 'is there any among you who knows the rider?' 'There is not, Lord,' said they. 'Let one of you go and meet her,' said he, 'to find out who she is'. One arose, but when he came onto the road to meet her, she had gone past. He followed her as fast as he could on foot, but the greater was his speed, all the further was she from him. And when he saw that it was idle for him to follow her he returned to Pwyll and said to him, 'Lord,' said he, 'it is idle for anyone in the world to follow her on foot.' 'Aye,' said Pwyll, 'go to the court and take the fleetest horse thou knowest and go after her.'

He took the horse and off he went. He came to the open level plain and showed the horse his spurs; and the more he pricked on his horse, all the further was she from him. Yet she held to the same pace as that she had started with. His horse flagged, and when he knew of his horse that its speed was failing, he returned to where Pwyll was. 'Lord,' said he, 'it is idle for anyone to follow yonder lady. I knew of no horse in the kingdom fleeter than that, but it was idle for me to follow her.' 'Aye,' answered Pwyll, 'there is some magic meaning there. Let us go towards the court.'

*

They came to the court, and they spent that night in song and carousal, so that they were well content. And on the morrow they beguiled the day until it was time to go to meat. And when their meat was ended Pwyll said, 'Where is the company we were yesterday, at the top of the mound?' 'We are here, lord,' said they. 'Let us go to the mound,' said he,' to sit'. 'And do thou,' said he to his groom, 'saddle my horse well and bring him to the road, and fetch with thee my spurs.' The groom did so. They came to the mound to sit; they had been there but a short while when they could see the rider coming by the same road, and in the same guise, and at the same pace. 'Ha, lad,' said Pwyll, 'I see the rider. Give me my horse.' Pwyll mounted his horse, and no sooner had he mounted his horse than she passed him by. He turned after her and let his horse, mettled and prancing, take its own speed. And he thought that at the second bound or the third he would come up with her. But he was no nearer to her than before. He drove his horse to its utmost speed, but he saw that it was idle for him to follow her.

Then Pwyll spoke. 'Maiden,' said he, 'for his sake whom thou lovest best, stay for me.' 'I will, gladly,' said she, 'and it had been better for the horse hadst thou asked this long since.' The maiden stayed and waited, and drew back that part of her headdress which should be over her face, and fixed her gaze upon him, and began to converse with him. 'Lady,' he asked, 'whence comest thou, and where art thou going?' 'I go mine own errands,' said she, 'and glad I am to see thee'.

'My welcome to thee! said he. And then he thought that the countenance of every maiden and every lady he had ever seen was unlovely compared with her countenance. 'Lady,' said he, 'wilt thou tell me anything of thine errands?' 'I will, between me and God,' said she. 'My main errand was to try to see thee.' 'That,' said Pwyll, 'is to me the most pleasing errand thou couldst come on. And wilt thou tell me who thou art?' 'I will, Lord,' said she. 'I am Rhiannon daughter of

Hefeydd the Old, and I am being given to a husband against my will. But no husband have I wished for, and that out of love of thee, nor will I have him even now unless thou reject me. And it is to hear thy answer to that that I come.' 'Between me and God,' replied Pwyll, 'this is my answer to thee – that if I had a choice of all the ladies and maidens in the world, 'tis thou I would choose.' 'Why,' said she, 'if that is thy will, before I am given to another man, make thou a tryst with me.' 'The sooner it be,' said Pwyll, 'the better for my part; and wherever thou wilt, make the tryst.'

Anon., 11th century
(tr. Gwyn Jones and Thomas Jones)

SUMMER

Epithalamion

Singing, today I married my white girl
beautiful in a barley field.
Green on thy finger a grass blade curled,
so with this ring I thee wed, I thee wed,
and send our love to the loveless world
of all the living and all the dead.

Now, no more than vulnerable human,
we, more than one, less than two,
are nearly ourselves in a barley field –
and only love is the rent that's due
though the bailiffs of time return anew
to all the living but not the dead.

Shipwrecked, the sun sinks down harbours
of a sky, unloads its liquid cargoes
of marigolds, and I and my white girl
lie still in the barley – who else wishes
to speak, what more can be said
by all the living against all the dead?

Come then all you wedding guests:
green ghost of trees, gold of barley,
you blackbird priests in the field,
you wind that shakes the pansy head
fluttering on a stalk like a butterfly;
come the living and come the dead.

Listen flowers, birds, winds, worlds,
tell all today that I married
more than a white girl in the barley –
for today I took to my human bed
flower and bird and wind and world,
and all the living and all the dead.

Dannie Abse

Let's go to Barry Island...

Let's go to Barry Island, Maggie fach,
And give all the kids one day by the sea,
And sherbet and buns and paper hats,
And a rattling ride on the Figure Eight;
We'll have tea on the sands, and rides on the donkeys,
And sit in the evening with the folk of Cwm Rhondda,
Singing the sweet old hymns of Pantycelyn
When the sun goes down beyond the rocky islands.
Come on, Maggie fach, or the trains will be gone
Then the kids will be howling at home all day,
Sticky with dirt and gooseberry jam.
Leave the washing alone for today, Maggie fach,
And put on your best and come out to the sun
And down to the holiday sea.
We'll carry the sandwiches in a big brown bag
And leave our troubles behind for a day
With the chickens and the big black tips
And the rival soup-kitchens, quarrelling like hell.
Come, Maggie fach, with a rose on your breast
And an old Welsh tune on your little red lips,
And we'll all sing together in the Cardiff train
Down to the holiday sea.

Idris Davies

Design for a Quilt

First let there be a tree, roots taking ground
In bleached and soft blue fabric.
Into the well-aired sky branches extend
Only to bend away from the turned-back
Edge of linen where day's horizons end;

Branches symmetrical, not over-flaunting
Their leaves (let ordinary swansdown
Be their lining), which in the summertime
Will lie lightly upon her, the girl
This quilt's for, this object of designing;

But such, too, when deep frosts veneer
Or winds prise at the slates above her,
Or snows lie in the yard in a black sulk,
That the embroidered cover, couched
And applied with pennants of green silk,

Will still be warm enough that should she stir
To draw a further foliage about her
The encouraged shoots will quicken
And, at her breathing, midnight's spring
Can know new season as they thicken.

Feather-stitch on every bough
A bird, one neat French-knot its eye,
To sing a silent night-long lullaby
And not disturb her or disbud her.
See that the entwining motives run

In and about themselves to bring
To bed the sheens and mossy lawns of Eden;
For I would have a perfect thing
To echo if not equal Paradise
As garden for her true temptation:

So that in future times, recalling
The pleasures of past falling, she'll bequeath it
To one or other of the line,
Bearing her name or mine,
With luck I'll help her make beneath it.

John Ormond

In Morfudd's Arms

Praised beyond all Enids be
Lady Morfudd, my lovely.
I burn with more than a fire
From the torch-light of her hair,

And yet, her touch as it fell
Was almost-virgin-gentle.

Around my neck white arms went;
Her red lips were impatient.
That kind of kissing has come,
So more than mild, most seldom.
Her poet-prisoner, frail
In her wine-sweet body-gaol,
So I, though I do not tell
All truth of the miracle.

So, in the bonds of the bright
Of her arms, all snow-drift white,
She was imprisoning me
All courtly, lightly, gently.
Who would want to stir
Out of her hold and halter?
Who would want to move
Out of that lock-up love?

And how could a man do better
Than submit to this fetter,
These gyves, this white-snow-gentle
Link and loop of the circle,
Chain and charm of the shackle,
Feather-threat of the throttle,
Wrist-hold, kiss-bold tether
Keeping us close together?

Each man thinks he knows best
Of Arthur's loveliest–
Tegau of the golden breast,
Dyfyr of the golden hair,
Enid, the radiant girl,
Daughter of Yniwl the Earl.

But I, Dafydd the dark,
The swarthy one, soot-sallow,
The too black crow-skin fellow
Rise over them all, and follow
Companioned only with
My marvel, my Morfudd,
So follow, and so fare
Towards that wider air
Rimmed by the gold-white arc.

How bountiful! How blest!

Dafydd ap Gwilym
(tr. Rolfe Humphries)

Her Merriment

When I had met my love the twentieth time,
She put me to confession day and night:
Did I love women far above all things,
Or did the songs I make give more delight?

'Listen, you sweeter flower than ever smiled
In April's sunny face,' I said at last –
'The voices and the legs of birds and women
Have always pleased my ears and eyes the most.'

And saying this, I watched my love with care,
Not knowing would my words offend or please;
But laughing gaily, her delighted breasts
Sent ripples down her body to her knees.

W.H. Davies

The North Star

There wanders many a lighted star
That in the high vault burns,
And every star an orbit hath
And in that orbit turns.

There's one white star, of all the rounds
That wheel high overhead,
And it is hung on heaven's pole
And will not rise nor bed.

So too with me: my firmament
Its own white star reveals,
And every sphere my heaven holds
Round her fixed axis wheels.

*John Morris-Jones
(tr. Tony Conran)*

Outside the Registry Office

It stands in a gently shabby part of the city,
a sober cube of red brick, built for use;
outside, small girls are crouching, serious
about their business, picking the confetti

out of the litter. The sacred ritual
of their play keeps all customs, as is fit;
their bride will dress in something long and white,
a sheet most like, and speak a language full

of what the civil contract has put by,
the sacrament and circumstance of words,
like a man, a poet it might be, who discards
the litter, sifting out the mystery.

Sheenagh Pugh

The Song she Brought

Lady, this is no snappy lingo.
No radio or teevee has sung me this.
For all the ad-man says, the whiteness
in my sheets is you naked there.
Outside a few foggy grunts on the river
– how those boats low in the night uneased.

But not my fate, no affinity there.
Lady, Lady, sing again the song you brought
through muffling fog and black water.
Let the foghorn stick in the river's throat
all night, like a bone.
We two move easier.

Graham Allen

61

from: *A War Wedding*

She comes to him in the night.

But she is wise and waits until I sleep.
She will not touch the blindness from my eyes
Nor stroke the hair of silence on my loins
Nor bare her wistful breasts.
For first I must encounter
My dreaming German soldier.
And when my body falls away
Will come my useless saviour.

Ah! but I feel her gesture shiver
As she beckons in infinite space;
In the void of heaven and hell
She starts the shrivelled heart
Of the panting moon awake.
And I rise from the restless armies
That cough like huddled sheep.
I lay the soiled red tourniquet aside,
She lies within my sleep.
Her golden hair is freed
About me and the thirsty stars
Are shaken from the mantling tree
And light the dark bruised seed.
The unborn children are singing
As we sail softly homing

Alun Lewis

Put your Arms Around my Body...

Put your arms around my body
And feed upon my breast,
And let your sorrow fade away
Into the darkening west.

In this hollow of the moorland
Young man, lie down with me,
And lose the day and its squalor
In the swoon of ecstasy.

Forget for tonight the tumult
The malice and the fret,
And know of the balm of my body
And clasp me and forget.

The hills and the vales are silent
And silent the stars above,
And my bosom is warm and gentle,
Young man, lie down and love.

Idris Davies

News of a Marriage

The world's reflected smoothly in our eyes,
as I would smooth your hair,
anaesthetised.

Everyone's in love, muffled
in the magic wool of couples
or out of love already

in a shoddy cloth of quarrels
over the shining pots
of the domestic mysteries.

Away from the carpeted landscape, they say,
some people move as quick as fish
with the urgency of survival:

a lot of people have left on planes
some with good reason;
some are back

their suitcases crammed
with views of cities
and disappointments.

In the hollow silence of the carpeted landscape
we stand, each muttering a childish apprehension.
The stairs are mildewed with darkness.
You can imagine but you can go no further,

frightened of the news that never changes,
yet still might:
spontaneity belongs to others now,
the point in the campaign where the desertions begin.

Steve Griffiths

from: *Before the Crying Ends*

And she have undone your donkey jacket easy never mind the rain getting in ice cold where she opened up them buttons.

Holding in close. Pressing you tight against the baths wall. Feeling her shiver there in the dark till she sucks some warmth away from your body. Stretching up her face to kiss your neck. Her wet chilled cheeks moving to a smile you cannot see as you wrap her in closer. Nudging those lips towards yours. And making those lips wait as they part eager breathing quick for kissing. And this small sound coming from those lips making you brush them with your own. And holding her face in your hands which got deadened by work long ago. Feeling nothing much except the feel of their own hard skin. And the softness of hers. They feel her skin. And letting your two mouths meet damp and warm till you are numb and electrified half out of your skull. And wanting that.

With her pulling away sudden like she got to or die. And stroking your face. And staring. And staring and searching. And full of sad happy tears running mingling with that drizzle. And groaning in to kiss again. And again. And again till you think she will hurt her breasts from the pressing. And feeling her breathless.

Damn you.

Holding her gentle with one arm. Turning her half away. Letting her feel under your shirt for the heat of your flesh.

There is no end to this.

I must be with you.

I feel so awful.

I go out of my mind.

O I love you Ben.

With this drumming feeling of trespass all bunched nasty in the front of your mind. With this long low ache of violation bent bow-shaped through your insides. With them thinking valves clogged good and thick same as boozing for hours. Except you have definitely not boozed lately. And knowing as how no drink you ever took have laid you down so helpless in your brain.

And her body is thawed now against your own. Holding her tight. Possessive. Listening eyes closed to the wind noises snittering through the conifers bordering the baths. Feeling deceitful to the world but honest with each other. A private feeling. A shared agony. An ecstasy. A wrongness. And a love.

Will I see you tomorrow?

I been praying you are not on afternoons.

Say you are on nights.

Please God say you are.

I been working it out,
    I'm on nights.

I love you.

I love you.
    Tomorrow.
    On the hill.

Our hill.

Our lovely hill.
    I might bring you a present.
    I might let you give it to me.

And she is gone. And you don't question it. For you have learned not to say good-bye. Not to say hello. Nor any other words that waste the time you got when one day is worth a week. When one hour is worth a day. When one minute is worth an hour. When one second is worth a kiss.

John L. Hughes

Glint

This was no image that held me
With compelled response.

I saw no sorcery in the shape,
The pure of feature; this was no idol

But flesh and blood, mouth and hair,
Breasts, thighs – the stuff of clay

And feeble blood,
The lineage of the grass, the stirring corn,

All whose desire went
Quietly to earth,

Like seaweed in the drunken wave,
Like clouds in light.

– To see her, a luxury; a leaven
Everlastingly young, the glint of her.

Euros Bowen
(tr. Tony Conran)

Midsummer Night

You are asleep. Your skin
is the stretched surface of water
drawn tight by the full moon rising

The cold light strikes from your thighs
and the polished curve of your shoulder
till all my bones glow red-hot

I am at the mercy of my bones
until they are plunged, hissing
deep in that icy lake.

Paul Merchant

from: *The Mabinogion*

'Wilt though follow a different counsel?' asked Pryderi. 'I had need of counsel,' said Manawydan,'and what counsel is that?' 'The seven cantrefs of Dyfed were left to me,' said Pryderi, 'and Rhiannon, my mother, is there. I will bestow her upon thee, and authority over the seven cantrefs with her. And though thou hadst no territory save those seven cantrefs, there are not seven cantrefs better than they. My wife is Cigfa daughter of Gwyn Gloyw,' said he, 'and though the territory is mine in name, let the enjoyment thereof be thine and Rhiannon's; and hadst thou ever desired territory, maybe thou mightest have that.' 'I desire none, chieftain,' said he; 'God repay thee thy friendship.' 'The best friendship I can show shall be thine if though wilt have it.' 'I will, friend,' said he; 'God repay thee. And I will go with thee to see Rhiannon and to look on the territory.' 'Thou dost well,' he answered. 'I believe thou didst never listen to a lady of better converse than she. What time she was in her heyday, no lady was more comely than she; and even now thou shalt not be ill-pleased with her looks.'

They went on their way, and however long they were upon the road they came to Dyfed. A feast was prepared for them against their coming, at Arberth, and Rhiannon and Cigfa had made it ready. And then Manawydan and Rhiannon began to sit together and to converse, and with the converse his head and heart grew tender towards her, and he admired in his heart how he had never beheld a lady more graced with beauty and comeliness than she. 'Pryderi,' said he, 'I will abide by what thou didst say.' 'What saying was that?' asked Rhiannon. 'Lady,' said Pryderi, 'I have bestowed thee as wife upon Manawydan son of Llyr.' 'And I too will abide by that, gladly,' said Rhiannon. 'Gladly will I too,' said Manawydan, 'and God repay the man who gives me his friendship as steadfastly as that.'

Before that feast ended he slept with her.

Anon., 11th century
(tr. Gwyn Jones and Thomas Jones)

Shirts

She hangs out his shirts,
pins them by the tails
to the singing line.

She hangs out his shirts,
and in the pure green
that the lawn paints them
she can see her face:
I am his wife.

In the attention
of cushions, the soft
elisions of a door –
a voice, her voice
comes back to her:
he is my husband,
I am his wife.

*I am the place
he returns to, his
hunger's home.
I build every day
a houseful of rooms,
of walls to enfold
the things that he loves.*

She hangs out his shirts,
and the air they breathe
fills them with flight:
his gentle arms rage
flailing at the sky,
scratching and clawing
to catch up with the wind.

She hangs out his shirts:
he is her husband,
she is his wife.

Nigel Jenkins

The World and Beti

(Lines in the Vale of Glamorgan)

1

In every tree in Glamorgan I see your beautiful face.
There where the leaves are a peacock your eyes follow.
I watch the bark forming your smile. The green beams of
    light
Pick you out on the waves of the air like chords on a harp;
And all the trees beyond Deheudir are moved by song,
Piling upon each other your tongues of mirth
Until they reach this spot an awdl of praise. The lore
Of your sap and sun is multiple through all the bounds of
    our province.
Beneath in Elai river I see your face again
Back and forth among the bubbles of water. Lord, the magic!
And quietly. Down among the reeds. Tadpoles there
Move through your purity. My wandering darling,
Your telegenity is televised at me through every minute:
Let the same media carry my love back.

2

Wherever I turn, I hoard your movements,
The way you move through a crowd, your bearing as you lay
Dishes on a table, your walk climbing stairs;
All are embroidered on my retina. To me
The turn of your elbow is such that I would be accounted
    foolish
If I spoke of the memory that comes for me here in Pendoylan.
There is no curlew and his cascade nor thrush and his
    fountain
That does not draw you to me, that doesn't sing of your
    nature.

Once we were joined; you are my treasure.
I am your burden; you are my support.
I am your poor barn; you are my door-keeper.
You are the upper reaches of the vale which flows with milk
    and honey;
I am the solitary place where you were lost. And you,
You are all my people. My reality and my illusion.

Bobi Jones

Aubade

At the first strain of waking, your face turns
And dives back innocently to its dark haunts,
The depths charged in the current of your dreams.
Lie there still, lie still.

Your eyes flicker like a screen: you glide
Serene in unfathomed waters and dip, live
As a fuse, through wrecked loves, their stories locked
And laved in turbulent holds.

Touch me, the last crusted captain who sparks
And crackles in your cold streams. Your breath
Flares, and we are iron ghosts that rise
Within the sound of sleep.

Eyes draw open. Hauled through the grey
Waves' scanned crest, our shadows explode,
Night has trawled us in its net and, landed,
We lie silver and gasping.

Robert Walton

Life Class

Here is my arm. My weight rests
lightly, poised and yielding
to take the load of my body
while letting the blood flow;
so when the tingle begins I can
shift a little, imperceptibly
without spoiling your view of the lines
the angles and shadows.
I watch the texture of light
on the slopes of my arm, and regard
its landscape, as if for the first time.

Here are my legs. Doubled up
my knees may present problems
of perspective. My thighs plunge
highlighted against the floor.
My trapped calves throb a little.
Soon the pain will start
to needle and stab, and I'll
breathe in rhythm, alongside,
keeping my distance.

Here is my stomach. There's a twist
in this posture, a challenge:
I am all changing planes.
The one part of me
that's visibly moving, rising
and falling as I breathe:
my belly, my centre
that cannot be still.
And my breasts, here, are just
two curves of light
and between my legs, a shadow.

Here is my head. I've tied
my hair so the stem of my neck
shows, the precise tilt,

the line between spine and brain.
I've turned my face aside
in abstraction. I prefer no
eye-contact: it jolts me back
into your world, the world
of touch and movement.
So I arrange my gaze
on a picture, a fragment of curtain,
two wood-knots, the flesh of my arm.

A long, slow time. The scratch
and shirr of pencils on paper
charcoal's thick squeak and whisper
clatter of brushes in water
subdued words, coughs and sighs
entertain me. I feed my mind
on all that concentration.

And yet it empties itself
constantly, it can't hold
to any thought, it must move –
or I can't keep still. It turns
and shifts, it is shrouded,
veiled, you can't draw it,
it's not available. My body
is public as the body of a tree
but my mind's private, goes
walkabout, darts like a bird.

Though there's one thought
returning, over and over.
How am I shameless
before strangers, before
their intimate gaze, yet
when my lover said, Stand up –
walk round the room; I want
to look at you – yes turn
like that...why did I blush
move stiffly, rapidly,
and cover myself with laughter?

Hilary Llewellyn-Williams

Watering the Flowers

I turn to speak
and you are watering the flowers:
by summer lamplight
spilling water from a yellow bowl

Great globes of silver shatter out and drop,
shimmering fall
through all the levels
of the leaves

I watch you stoop:
shadowy arms and shoulders, hair
cascading
on the dusky blooms

In garden after garden
blossoms droop –
out to the suburbs
and beyond

Meadows lie deep
Children sleep
while you are watering the flowers

Sepal and ovule ache
You will not stop until
each petal swollen with the weight
bows down

dust turns to nectar
worlds are dripping in your wake

                    Alan Perry

from: *Young Emma*

Louise had now been with me a little over a year, and then the end came suddenly. She was taken ill, and in bed for three months. During that time I waited patiently for her, without a thought of other women. But when she was able to walk and came to see me, it was only to say that she was not coming back, and that all must now be over between us. The man she was living with had been so good to her that she had no intention of being false to him again. 'Although there is no great love on his part or mine,' she said – 'we like each other well enough to make things pleasant.'

When I heard this, I said nothing, for I knew it would all be for the best in the end. But Louise broke down and cried, when we parted at last. As for me, I went back upstairs and, lying on the bed, was in half a stupor for several hours. But when Louise did not come the next morning, after breakfast, it was then that I suffered most; especially when so many little things came under my notice, to remind me of her care, which I would no longer have.

'If I ever leave you,' she had said once – 'you will say, "What a good friend was Louise!" and be sorry you have lost me.'

Have these words come true, and do I think of Louise now? While I write these words, I am a married man, and happy; but we will leave that matter alone for the present – my brain must not work faster than my hand. But there is one thing in my house, which comes under my eyes every day; and I have only to look at it and I must think of Louise. It is a bronze bust of myself, done by a good sculptor, and full of life. The life in the lips is almost uncanny, and full of fascination. But when strangers or friends come to my house and praise the life-like quality of that bronze mould, a great lump rises in my throat, which is not caused by pride in possessing so fine a work of art, or its commercial value. One time, when I went wandering away from home, I had left Louise in charge, to come every day, in my absence, to see that everything was all right, and to keep the place clean. I was away for over a month and, when I returned, there was a welcome glow in her eyes; and everything seemed to be in its proper place, as clean and bright as her own self. But the next day, when I happened to look at my bronze head, I saw, to my surprise, that although the lips were dark and clean, yet, for all that, the nose, the eyebrows and the hair were white with dust. I could not account for this, seeing that the lips, which were so clean, protruded in the same way as the nose and the eyebrows, and were just as likely to catch the dust. However, although I thought the matter was strange, I did not think it was of sufficient interest to brood over, and dismissed the subject at once. But about three or four days after this, when Louise was in a happy mood, she pointed to my bronze head, and said in a shy, low voice – 'I came here every morning, when you were away, and never failed once: and the very first thing I did, when I entered the room, was to kiss that mouth!' So, every time I look at my Bronze head, I think of the time when that hard mouth was kept clean by living lips.

Louise has gone, and it is hardly likely that I shall ever see her again; but this truth remains with me to the end of my days. She was the first woman that ever had any real affection for me.

W.H. Davies

Poem from Llanybri

If you come my way that is...
Between now and then, I will offer you
A fist full of rock cress fresh from the bank
The valley tips of garlic red with dew
Cooler than shallots, a breath you can swank.

In the village when you come. At noon-day
I will offer you a choice bowl of cawl
Served with a 'lover's' spoon and a chopped spray
Of leeks or savori fach, not used now,

In the old way you'll understand. The din
Of children singing through the eyelet sheds
Ringing 'smith hoops, chasing the butt of hens;
Or I can offer you Cwmcelyn spread

With quartz stones from the wild scratchings of men:
You will have to go carefully with clogs
Or thick shoes for it's treacherous the fen,
The East and West Marshes also have bogs.

Then I'll do the lights, fill the lamp with oil,
Get coal from the shed, water from the well;
Pluck and draw pigeon with crop of green foil
This your good supper from the lime-tree fell.

A sit by the hearth with blue flames rising,
No talk. Just a stare at 'Time' gathering
Healed thoughts, pool insight, like swan sailing
Peace and sound around the home, offering

You a night's rest and my day's energy.
You must come – start this pilgrimage
Can you come? – send an ode or elegy
In the old way and raise our heritage.

Lynette Roberts

from: *Country Dance*

The master is ploughing. The crows follow the furrow, flying round him, and settling on the red earth where he has passed.

His eyes are on his work; only at the turn he sees me stood watching him in the shadow of the hedge, and as he moves down the field his words come back to me, though they are softly spoken in the tongue he was born to:

'What art thou doing there all alone?'

It is the truth that I answer:

'Waiting for thee.'

It is dark when he leaves the plough and, coming to me, looks down in my face:

'Fy nghariad, the waiting is over,' he says, and with his two hands draws me to him.

Margiad Evans

Swallows

Steps on the creaking stairs
set panicking a nestful
of young swallows in an empty room,
their little bodies hurtling
through dead air to dirty window-panes.

'This shall be a quiet room', said the man
to his gipsy delicate girl, who gently
gathered swallows into her thin hands.
'We'll walk barefoot, keep silence here', he planned.
'Look!' she said, rapt, holding out to him
a tiny brittle swallow in each hand.

But it was only the future
that he could see, and while he paced
its hopeful rooms, she opened the window
and set the moment free to go
on soft wings into summer and the past.

Ruth Bidgood

Inns of Love

You are my Anchor and my Ship,
my Porto Bello, my Welcome to Town,
my Swan, my Angel, my White Hart,
my Bunch of Grapes, my Salutation.

May I be Crown to your fresh Rose,
the Falcon for your Crystal Palace,
a leaping Dolphin to your Star
and to your Albion, Prince of Wales.

A Unicorn to your World's End,
in your sweet Valley I'll be Trout,
Hound to your Hare, I'm the Green Man
will hold you in his Western Arms.

Gwyn Williams

from: *Mel's Secret Love*

Dear Mel,
  I am writing this note to ask you to marry me. I know that
the house at Corn Hir is not in good condition as at present,
but I am quite prepared to make any alterations you would
want should you agree to my proposal. As you know Corn Hir
is a very productive unit. You may not know that I have a sub-
stantial bank balance in the region of ten thousand five hun-
red pounds, also five thousand in the war loan after my uncle
and three thousand unit trust investments. As you know I
have always felt very warmly towards you and I know it
would please your parents to have you near,

Your sincere friend,
John

When Winnie came back from the last bus she was full of enthusiasm for Judy's new home.

'You should have seen the kitchen, Mel. You would have loved it. Fridge, washing-machine, super cooker, food-mixer, the lot. She's got it made, girl. All she does is wander around the house polishing her wedding presents. I can tell you, love, I was mad with envy. And he's quite nice too. Quiet you know and can't do too much for her. It's the only thing you know, Mel, in the end. At the end of the day, as old Harold says, you put the cat out and lock the door, up to slumberland and hear him snore.'

Winnie hooted with laughter. Mel, who was in her dressing-gown and ready for bed, handed Winnie John's letter to read. Winnie opened her mouth wide and flattened her hand against her breast.

'Mel! This is a proposal!'

'Look at the way he's written it,' Mel said. 'He's so ignorant. He annoys me. Now I'll have to write him an answer. It's very embarrassing.'

'What's it like, Mel?'

'It's a dump. Stuck up in the hills, overlooking a river. Pigs everywhere and poultry. Ponies and sheep in the garden. Old bedsteads in the hedges. It's such a mess. You've never seen anything like it. Hasn't even got indoor sanitation. He's got some cheek, I must say.'

Winnie had become serious as Mel was talking. She lit a cigarette and waved away the smoke.

'You know what I think, Mel? Do you mind if I speak quite frankly? If I were you I'd accept him.'

'Accept him!'

Mel was as indignant as if Winnie had insulted her.

'You've had a bad time, Winnie said. I'm your friend and I wouldn't be a good friend if I didn't tell you. What's gone is gone, but what about the future? We'll have to get out of here very soon now and where will we go? Point number one. We're not getting any younger. Point number two. We're not well paid. Point number three. He may be a bit of a hillbilly, but he's got the cash and that's what counts. We can't live on romance forever. We've had our fling and now's the time to settle down...'

'You marry him then!'

Mel snatched a cigarette and furrowed her forehead.

'I would like a shot if he asked me. You're the romantic type, Mel. And you want to watch out. There's nothing wrong these days living in the country. You'll have a car of your own. And the telly. Put central heating in...'

Winnie picked up John's letter and read,

'"Any alterations you would want"! Take out the war loan and you could build another house in the next field, Mel. You accept him. Don't be daft. This is a wonderful chance. You take it.'

'He's got a nerve,' Mel said. 'Writing to me like that.'

'Any woman can train a man if she puts her mind to it', Winnie said. 'Look at Judy. She's got her bank-clerk sitting up and begging. You could do just the same if you wanted to.'

'Well I don't want to...'

'Sleep on it,' Winnie said. 'Sleep on my words and take my advice. Say "Yes" first thing in the morning. Don't give him a chance to change his mind.'

Emyr Humphreys

Violet

Violet was the colour of the waters I knew in the
far-off days,
Pwll Du, Pwll y Merched, Pownd Cwar
the easeful lakes
that embraced our sweaty bodies
like experienced women,
and that cooled our young enthusiasm
in their ready arms
in the June of our need
                    long ago.

Violet was the colour of the secure hilltops
that guarded our valley,
Pen y Clogau, y Garreg Fraith, Penllerfedwen.
These like patient mothers
breast-nursed our tired griefs
and we whispered to them our careful secrets
in the nights of our need
                    long ago.

Violet was the colour of the warm stones
in the walls of the friendly farmhouses.
Y Lluest, Bryn Hyfryd, y Foel.
In their shadow
the tentative rhythms, flesh to flesh,
and kisses and whitehot promises.
These are the stones we humanised,
on the summer nights of our need
                    long ago.

Feminine violet,
your tint remains in the waters
on the hilltops and the stones,
transfiguring and warming them
as it did
                    long summers ago.

Bryan Martin Davies
(tr. R. Gerallt Jones)

The Way of It

With her fingers she turns paint
into flowers, with her body
flowers into a remembrance
of herself. She is at work
always, mending the garment
of our marriage, foraging
like a bird for something
for us to eat. If there are thorns
in my life, it is she who
will press her breast to them and sing.

Her words, when she would scold,
are too sharp. She is busy
after for hours rubbing smiles
into the wounds. I saw her,
when young, and spread the panoply
of my feathers instinctively
to engage her. She was not deceived,
but accepted me as a girl
will under a thin moon
in love's absence as someone
she could build a home with
for her imagined child.

R.S. Thomas

Light Breaks where no Sun Shines

Light breaks where no sun shines;
Where no sea runs, the waters of the heart
Push in their tides;
And, broken ghosts with glow-worms in their heads,
The things of light
File through the flesh where no flesh decks the bones.

A candle in the thighs
Warms youth and seed and burns the seeds of age;
Where no seed stirs,
The fruit of man unwrinkles in the stars,
Bright as a fig;
Where no wax is, the candle shows its hairs.

Dawn breaks behind the eyes;
From poles of skull and toe the windy blood
Slides like a sea;
Nor fenced, nor staked, the gushers of the sky
Spout to the rod
Divining in a smile the oil of tears.

Night in the sockets rounds,
Like some pitch moon, the limit of the globes;
Day lights the bone;
Where no cold is, the skinning gales unpin
The winter's robes;
The film of spring is hanging from the lids.

Light breaks on secret lots,
On tips of thought where thoughts smell in the rain;
When logics die,
The secret of the soil grows through the eye,
And blood jumps in the sun;
Above the waste allotments the dawn halts.

Dylan Thomas

Four Letters

Lloyd George to Frances Stevenson

8 August 1915

My own sweet little Pussy

I am longing to be back with you. I am becoming more intolerant of these partings month by month. I cannot live now without my darling. I know that better even than I did weeks ago. It is either you or nothing for me *Cariad.*

I have had the dreariest of holidays – rain mist damp. Tonight I motor to Colwyn. I leave Colwyn at 9.19 tomorrow reaching Euston at 2.12 – then –

Now Pussy I have made up my mind to disappoint myself – you. I have two days of most important & trying work in front of me – conferences & decisions upon which the success of the Department depend & I must reserve all my strength for them. I know you will agree. Wednesday we can go to Walton. Meanwhile help me to restrain myself – for I am lost for my passion for you is a *consuming* flame – it burns up all wisdom prudence & judgment in my soul. Help me *cariad bach anwyl aur.*

I feel as if during the last two months I have not given my very best to the terrible task entrusted to me. My future depends entirely on it. What is much more important – the nation's future depends on it. The distracting events of the past few weeks have half paralysed me & I must pull myself together. I cannot do so without your wise help. You are everything to me now. My failure or success will depend entirely on you. You possess my soul entirely.

Tomorrow night I dine with Churchill so you can make your own arrangements.

Oh I do want to see you – I want *you* & no one & nothing else.

Your own
D. – for ever

*

23 August 1915   The Grand
                                        Folkestone

My own sweet child
I received both your darling letters & they were like nectar
for lips parched with a great passion. I have been these 2 or
3 days thinking things of unutterable tenderness & love for
my little *cariad*. My affection for her has deepened & sweet-
ened beyond anything words can tell. Yours is the tenderest
and purest love of my life Pussy *bach anwyl aur*. I could face
anything with you. I have been thinking of you all day &
much of the night & always oh so fondly.
Returning tomorrow. No time to write anymore. I love my
pure little darling.

                              Ever & Ever
                              Your own
                                   D.

*

13th August 1925   Criccieth

My girl
Am off to see the annual sheep trial. Do you remember? 14
years ago. I was stricken then & the disease has obtained
complete hold of me body & soul. Worst of all I like it – yes I
do my own darling little rascal.
Delighted to get your letter – full of your doings. It is what
I wanted to know. You are doing just what I want. Get well.
You will need every ounce of your strength.
This is the 7th day. I count off one by one.
Write *tomorrow*. I loved your letter today. Just the stuff for
me.
Fond fond affection love tenderness & *Naughtiness*
                              Ever & Ever
                                   D.

Love to Muriel. Tell her to cut in at once if she sees you flirt-
ing.

*

12 August 1927

Frances Stevenson *is* & will always remain the sweetie of Davy Lloyd.

Blue Carnations

Oh no, it is *I* who have the sense of direction,
And it is *you* who are good with maps. And yet,
Much more patient than you think you are, much
More generous than you claim I can be, you put
Up with my loud assertions, laugh when you are right.

And it occurs to me that since our early days
Together, I have always been following the maps
You have sketched and that my sense of direction
Tells me only how to find you and it is always you
Who really knows where we are and how not to be lost.

I shall go on blustering, making you laugh;
And teasing you when you pretend to be careless.
But your maps make sense and meaning of our world:
And I am happy to go on walking until I find
Blue carnations or any other token of loving you.

Stuart Evans

Choughs

I follow you downhill to the edge
My feet taking as naturally as yours
To a sideways tread, finding footholds
Easily in the turf, accustomed
As we are to a sloping country.

The cliffs buttress the bay's curve to the north
And here drop sheer and sudden to the sea.
The choughs plummet from sight then ride
The updraught of the cliffs' mild yellow
Light, fold, fall with closed wings from the sky.

At the last moment as in unison they turn
A ripcord of the wind is pulled in time.
He gives her food and the saliva
Of his red mouth, draws her black feathers, sweet
As shining grass across his bill.

Rare birds that pair for life. There they go
Divebombing the marbled wave a yard
Above the spray. Wings flick open
A stoop away
From the drawn teeth of the sea.

Gillian Clarke

AUTUMN

In September

Again the golden month, still
Favourite, is renewed;
Once more I'd wind it in a ring
About your finger, pledge myself
Again, my love, my shelter,
My good roof over me,
My strong wall against winter.

Be bread upon my table still
And red wine in my glass; be fire
Upon my hearth. Continue,
My true storm door, continue
To be sweet lock to my key;
Be wife to me, remain
The soft silk on my bed.

Be morning to my pillow,
Multiply my joy. Be my rare coin
For counting, my luck, my
Granary, my promising fair
Sky, my star, the meaning
Of my journey. Be, this year too,
My twelve months long desire.

John Ormond

Field of Wheat

Out from the storming night they came
and before them the field bowed
over to the sky and fell towards the sea.
Rich and gold the wheat settled like hair
though the facing slope was shadowed at its centre.

    See, how the wheat is broken and flattened there
    she said – that must have been the storm.
    But then, why just at that point?

He said – that's a fox after a hare,
some hunted creature flushed from cover.

    No! I want an older spirit,
    Branwen, daughter of Llyr, escaped from Ireland
    and running across a Welsh field.

He turned back into the room – some freak
of wind, some current eddying down.
This room's a mess. Let's tidy up.

    No wind's scythe, but two lovers thrashing
    in the field – she said
    as we have done.

He shook down the quilt with peacocks
– Stay close to me in my life, you
and your imagination.

                    Tony Curtis

Moving House Again

I should be used to it now,
To all the circumstance,
The first shock of knowing,
And after, the slow destruction, the empty rooms.

Still, like the caddis-fly,
I hoard stray ornaments,
The key from an altered lock,
A table-cloth,
Brass holders that lost their piano years ago.
After another or another move
These too will be left behind.

If love be evicted too,
By distance or death,
How long before memories,
Of no further use,
Are left in the empty room
With the old clock that does not go?

Sally Roberts Jones

from: *The Scandalous Thoughts*
of Elmyra Mouth

He repeated a family joke. 'It's not the drink, Auntie, it's the company.'

'I can see that by the veins on your nose.'

'Go on...' he gave her a playful squeeze.

'Stay if you want,' she kept her hands behind his neck.

'No, I can't. It's Fred's last night.'

She bared her teeth and released him. Men, she thought; animals. If he didn't come up the stairs cat-footed, she'd turn the tap off that night. Shut shop it would be, him and his drink and his Fred! As her mother'd advised, there was such a thing as frostbite after closing. But like her mother, she didn't want to be thought a bad old sort. So she merely grunted; 'Get on with you. And come home with more than your bracers!'

When he had gone, she heard the familiar clunk of the car's gears outside and lit a cigarette before getting the children to bed. There was nothing for her on the telly as usual. With all the money they spent on it, you'd think there might be a show she'd actually enjoy now and again. Sometimes there was a serial or a play with which she could identify, but it was never from Wales and usually had to do with the Midlands or the North. Locally, she did not count, she supposed. Not that she gave a monkey's. Davie said you had to go to Bristol to get the Welsh edition of the Radio Times because nobody took it locally. But why should they? It had precious little to do with them, any more than it did the other commercial lot, who weren't even worth mentioning except for a passing sigh for the Dorchester film stars worrying about South Wales on their yachts. Who was kidding who? They were no bottle from the start. Mouths shut, remember the divi, and don't offend Bristol again. Where were the valleys in that?

She finished her cigarette and went up to inspect the bathroom which Davie had recently tiled. It contained a coloured bath, pink, with matching accessories, and a luxury of luxuries, a separate shower attachment. Elmyra could remember what it was like not to have a proper bathroom and she thought her coloured suite a whizz and no mistake. Now she looked proudly at the hand towels, the matching floor mat and lavatory cover, and thanked God for Embassy coupons. It was the most hallowed room in the house.

Presently, she called the children in, and having bathed them and settled them down in their nightdresses, decided to bathe herself. If Davie but knew it, she spent hours in the bathroom, wallowing in the suds, endlessly combing her hair, and surveying herself in the long mirror she'd insisted upon. She often took her measurements. Two kids and hardly an inch on or off at either end. Boy, she was too good to waste, she thought. It was a good job she was faithful. There were always plenty of chances. She couldn't go down the market Saturdays without what seemed like a visiting team trying to look down her dress, but she'd developed a look that killed, she fondly imagined. And anyway, she wasn't interested. They said a slice off a cut loaf was never missed, but not her loaf, thank you very much. She was took, a one-man woman.

She did not dress after her bath, slipped a robe on and went downstairs where she attempted to read her horoscope from a woman's journal, but somehow she couldn't concentrate. She didn't know quite what it was, but her mind was on the itch. Was their marriage getting boring? Did they take each other too much for granted? She'd caught Davie looking at pin-ups a lot lately, his eye flashing to the ripe page of the *Mirror* before he so much as crackled a cornflake. What if his eye was beginning to wander elsewhere?

At first, she put the thought out of her mind and turned to the broken hearts column which she also read avidly. People's troubles were incredible. The best required a stamped addressed envelope for a confidential reply, but she was adept at reading between the lines. Some men were so crooked, they'd fox their own shadows. And slimy with it, pure slime. But not her Davie. She couldn't understand how she even gave it a thought. He was as good as gold always. As open as the day is long.

And yet it nagged, this thought. For some reason, her natural confidence began to ebb away. It was the BBC that did it.

Of course, it was ridiculous and the Cardiff lot were nothing like the London lot in any respect, but it was the showbiz world even if most of it was all in Welsh. Oh, why couldn't he get a job in the chain works or on the trading estate? Why couldn't he get a job at home? They said travel broadened the mind, even twelve miles a day, but there was all the difference in the world in those twelve miles leading down to Cardiff. She saw them stretching out in her mind's eye, Treforest, the Estate, Taff's Well, Whitchurch, and then the environs of the capital city opening up like the red light district in some lurid American film. Downtown What-You-Call, she thought. She'd give him Downtown! Bloody Cardiff....It was so cold compared to the valleys. Oh, why couldn't he get a job at home?

Then suddenly, her mind began to panic. It was as if a spring had begun to unwind, a coil slipping slowly from its point of tension, then exploding, thoughts expanding like rings of steel and spilling into every corner of her mind.

What if he was on the knock? All those stories about Malay girls. What did they call them? Taxi Dancers. And what about the divorces in showbiz? The Boss of the whole BBC had had one and now he was working for the commercials! There was no such thing as bloody loyalty any more. You only had to sit in that canteen to listen to them tearing each other's programmes apart to know that. Everybody got stick, and the South Wales boys who were coining it on 'Z cars' in London got the most. That was one thing, another was that she'd refused to go to the Christmas party on principle. The poor bloody technicians always got the raw end of it with the bilingual production staff and the bigwigs ruling the roost. She didn't fancy being squeezed, pawed or patronised in that crush. It was like Machynlleth zoo. If they had a zoo in Machynlleth. And if they did, Glamorgan and Monmouthshire people had to pay for it. Like the bloody language. And as for what went on down in Make-Up after some of those *Ychafi* programmes, disgusting wasn't the word. Sometimes, they had actors there, and actresses, and the Make-Up girls said anything went. It was no good putting in to see Controller (Wales) either because he said London was worse and Glasgow the best, according to what somebody had told somebody who told Davie. At any rate, it was no place for a self-respecting valley girl. Even if they didn't have queers which Davie said were everywhere else. Like some places he knew where you had to stand with your back to the wall as soon as you got into the lift, by all accounts.

But what about Davie? If Fred What's-His-Name was on transfer to *Panorama*, he'd be ready to let himself go, wouldn't he? They'd probably have the riggers out drinking with them, and the scene shifters, and there was a commissionaire who could tell a story or two, she knew about them. Once they got the beer into them, there'd be no telling what they'd do. If they weren't at it with the Welshy lot, they might be down the docks and that was almost as bad, if not quite. The trouble was, once you got near Cardiff, the values changed. You could get drunk up the valleys like a man, but after stop-tap, home you had to come, boyo, one foot behind the other, or no place for you but the gutter. And there was something very comforting about the gutter. There was seldom room for two in it.

But Cardiff, the docks....She thought about them obsessionally now. What she hated most was her sense of the city's anonymity, those cold wide streets, actual architecture, people pushing, sometimes stuck-ups with yet another accent and the girls in the better shops trying to sound like a lot of lezzes and looking down their nose at you if you ever had to leave your address.

'Dan y Graig Street and up yours too!'

What was good about the valleys from her present point of view was that there was many a fly that was never unbuttoned because it would be all over town the next day. You couldn't bend down to straighten your tights without half the street pricing your under-clothes. Walls had ears and bricks had eyes, and it was a good job too, made you feel part of the family, and keeping the old Adam down in all but the wilder spirits and they were usually Poles or County School boys. There was no creeping off and having it on the sly if you were married unless you were the Invisible Man or something. What worried her now was the thought of them all together, egging each other on. They said there were some rugby clubs who actually had a competition when they went on the Cornish tour. Who'd be the first of the married men to click! Thank Gawd for that Malayan terrorist anyhow! He'd put the shot in just the right place.

By eleven- thirty, Elmyra was convinced that her marriage was threatened. If it could happen to Diana Dors, it could happen to her, couldn't it? They must be on the razzle. Must be.

As a matter of principle, she never kept drink in the house, except at Christmas. It was not that nobody called, but rather, that she knew very well who might call, and the men there were around here, you couldn't give them one drink. Oh, no. With them, it was one drink, finish the bottle. They were as Welsh as Welsh in that, out-and-outers, the bloody lot of them. It so happened that there was a half bottle of rum which her father had given Davie for his chest in the winter. She brought it out and poured herself a liberal tot and drank it with a swallow. She'd give him a going-over when he came in. If there was a hint of another woman, she'd give him a beating, the like of which the street had never known. There'd been some famous cases, one erring husband sewn in bed sheets and laced with a broom handle in his cups, another wrapped up in wet wallpaper and pasted all over like a snowman before he got his. They didn't believe in sulking, the Dan y Graig women. Defiantly, she poured another tot, swallowed it, and then another. She'd give him sox!

But by one o'clock when there was still no sign of him, her rage turned like the weather cock to self pity. She was drunk now, wallowing in remorse. All these accusations. It was her fault, she'd refused to move to Cardiff in the first place. What was the good of blaming him if he didn't have a home handy? All the temptations were put in his way. He was a boy-and-a-half as far as his attractions went. A wife's place was to follow her husband. She'd jibbed at the first thing he'd ever really asked her. And now what was she doing? Never a quitter be, her father always said, true to the pit always; neither a quitter nor a squealer. Now she was both.

By two o'clock she'd finished the bottle. She got to her feet and staggered to bed. Now she was maudlin, disaster's vicitm. Dead, she thought, he was dead, neatly incised on the motorway, or crushed under some truck. He'd told her once he'd seen a man cut in half by a lengthy burst from a sten gun, actually in half. Now she transferred the image to her own mind, but it was too horrible. He was normally the most careful of drivers, but then, they were the sort who always copped it. She could not remember going upstairs or what she did when she got there, but she already saw herself as a widow, pale and grief-stricken in black with the entire street turned out for the funeral and perhaps a sight of one or two of the BBC celebrities who might be there. It was all over in her mind. Perhaps they'd fiddle it to say that he was working so she'd get a pension, no doubt Controller (Wales) would find a few words of English to cheer her up, but she was a widow all right. She *felt* like a widow. Thank Gawd her grandmother's left her the house. She sobbed herself to sleep finally, lying naked on the coverlet, her long, black hair hanging down by the side of the bed.

It was in this position that Davie found her at three o'clock in the morning. He smelt the rum on her breath with some annoyance. There was no call for that, nothing wrong with her chest, but he said nothing, stripped and eased himself in beside her, taking care to throw the coverlet over her in case she would catch a chill.

In the morning, it was he who attacked first.

'You were lying there looking like a bloody book jacket. What if the children had come in?'

She felt dreadful, a mouth like a birdcage. Her temples throbbed as she looked at him blearily. She'd decided on something before she fell asleep, but now she could not remember what it was.

'You said twelve...'

'I was late because I had to drive everybody else home.'

'Twelve, you said.'

'Well I wasn't much after, but before you go on at me, have you seen the bathroom?'

'The bathroom?' she caught at her throat. She had a vague memory of disturbance, a sense of sin.

'Were you swinging on the light cord, or what?'

'Swinging?'

'The plaster's flaked on the ceiling by the switch, and the matching accessories are stuffed down the pan.'

'The pan?'

'The lav,' he said accusingly. 'What did you have, an orgy all on your own?'

In her frenzy, she must have tried to wreck her own creation! *Ychafi!* And even as he accused, the fact that he did not couple her with anyone else shamed her all the more. Thoughts was awful things when you came to think of them: nasty.

'Oh, lor'...Sorry kid,' she said guiltily.

'I should think so too.'

She though for a moment, then looked at him. 'It's the bloody BBC. I get worried. I don't know why you don't try and get a job at home.'

He looked at her startled.

'Hey?'

Then she said what everybody knew and Honours Graduates denied: 'You know you won't get on there. It's all clicks, and with your *shoni's* Welsh, what chance?'

He said nothing. They had discussed the matter before and what she said was right. It was just that he was easy going.

But now she pursued it.

'A little photographer's or something?' she said suggestively, as only she could. She slanted her eyes in a look she privately called, The Japanese Goodnight. 'If you had a shop, you could come home dinner times. When the kids are in School. You know....'

He sighed. He knew the signs. From now on, she'd get her beak on it like a jackdaw at a nut. Might as well say yes to a shopkeeper before she dressed.

'We'll see,' he said comfortably. 'Leave it at that for the moment.'

'Great,' she said happily, and later a sweet, intimate poem in monosyllables: 'Oh...Oh...Oh, Duw-Duw! Oh, help! Oh, Malaya! Oh, smashing!'

Further up the steet where the houses had bay windows and the occasional colour television they said Elmyra Mouth was as common as dirt, but the most endearing thing about her was that she thought him, her husband, the most desirable man in all the world. He was hers, and apart from him and the children, she had but a single thought. 'If you was

from the valleys, stay in the valleys.' Nothing else made
sense.

Alun Richards

The Imitation Burtons

They sat in the corner seat.
She knew she looked like Liz.
Stared at herself in the pane.
Small nose, not quite black hair,
A loose coat – frankly, grubby.
Cleopatra's eyes her own.

Next to her sat hubby.
Not so certainly him.
But almost – a bull of a man
Strong though slightly balding,
A resonant quiet voice
And duffle-coat no doubt.

She snuggled next to him.
Was he her Dicky's dream?
Old eyes from celluloid
Transmuted to flesh then missed
Like all sod, earthy things.
(The Burtons know how it feels)

John Powell Ward

from: *Under Milk Wood*

Polly's Song

I loved a man whose name was Tom
He was strong as a bear and two yards long
I loved a man whose name was Dick
He was big as a barrel and three feet thick
And I loved a man whose name was Harry
Six feet tall and sweet as a cherry
But the one I loved best awake or asleep
Was little Willy Wee and he's six feet deep.

O Tom Dick and Harry were three fine men
And I'll never have such loving again
But little Willy Wee who took me on his knee
Little Willy Wee was the man for me.

Now men from every parish round
Run after me and roll me on the ground
But whenever I love another man back
Johnnie from the Hill or Sailing Jack
I always think as they do what they please
Of Tom Dick and Harry who were tall as trees
And most I think when I'm by their side
Of little Willy Wee who drowned and died.

O Tom Dick and Harry were three fine men
And I'll never have such loving again
But little Willy Wee who took me on his knee
Little Willy Weazel is the man for me.

Dylan Thomas

A Pregnant Woman

Today she parades her shape like swellings of song,
The wings that free her, her throne, her tower.
She bursts the land with her being, her objective, her
  blossom,
Her passion's lofty monument, her belly's dance.

The trickling that was a stream to her hope breaks through
  its banks,
Swirling in floods. Come, everyone out of the way.
Where's the tall mountain that will not be drowned?
What terror! Look at this. There's nothing loftier.

Along the length and the breadth of our fields the world
  makes its way.
Oh everyone, run to the side. She is spacious as time.
Watch out for your toes. She carries the stresses
Of the season's muse, her mite of a chick's hidden
  thumping.

And upon her face is the smile of the Almighty.
Who? Has anyone seen this fulfilling before?
On her tomorrow's sunny roof her rapture warbles:
It chirps, a live coal, in the twigs of her breast.

Cautious her step lest she trample the eggs of Creation,
Light her heart lest she weigh down the little one.
She walks, like Peter on water, doubtfully joyful,
Till she beaches her glory's pyramid in a dry Canaan.

                    Bobi Jones
                    (tr. Joseph Clancy)

He Whose Hand and Eye are Gentle

To tell you from the start, I have lost him whose hand and eye are gentle; I shall go to seek him of the slender eyebrows, wherever the most generous and fairest of men may be.

I shall go to the midst of Gwent without delaying, to the south I shall go to search, and charge the sun and the moon to seek for him whose hand and eye are gentle.

I shall search through all the lands, in the valley and on the mountain, in the church and in the market, where is he whose hand and eye are gentle.

Mark you well, my friends, where you see a company of gentlemen, who is the finest and most loving of them; that is he whose hand and eye are gentle.

As I was walking under the vine the nightingale bade me rest, and it would get information for me where was he whose hand and eye are gentle.

The cuckoo said most kindly that she herself was quite well informed, and would send her servant to inquire without ceasing where was he whose hand and eye are gentle.

The cock-thrush advised me to have faith and hope, and said he himself would take a message to him whose hand and eye are gentle.

The blackbird told me she would travel to Cambridge and to Oxford, and would not complete her nest till she found him whose hand and eye are gentle.

I know that he whose speech is pleasant can play the lute and play the organ; God gave the gift of every music to him whose hand and eye are gentle.

Hunting with hawks and hounds and horses, catching and calling and letting slip, none loves a slim dog or a hound like him whose hand and eye are gentle.

Anon., 16th century
(tr. Kenneth Hurlstone Jackson)

Sailing

It was very strange to watch him sail
Away from me on the calm water,
The white sail duplicate. I knew
All the people in the boat and felt
The tightening lines of my involvement.

My children were in the boat, and my friends,
And he in the stern. The sheet of water
Thinned between us as he sailed away.
I strolled on the path and waved
And felt in the space a terrible desolation.

When they returned the exhilaration
Of the familiar morning had gone. I felt
As though on the water he had found
New ways of evasion, a sheet
Of icy water to roll out between us.

Gillian Clarke

Separation

Sleeping by myself is curious.
The strangeness isn't the product
                                    of your not being here,
of the cold fact of disconnectedness –
but your refusal in our severance
                                    to be utterly away!

You persist on the edges of perception,
                                    a distraction –
an imaginary sound that turns my head,
a shadow half-glimpsed in mirror-glass,
the wraith of a perfume in the room.

Tonight I shall douse the light,
clamber into the emptiest of sheets,
                                    close my eyes,
and fold myself away into your absence.

                                    Richard Poole

Esyllt

As he climbs down our hill, my kestrel rises,
Steering in silence up from five empty fields,
A smooth sun brushed brown across his shoulders,
Floating in wide circles, his warm wings stiff.
Their shadows cut; in new soft orange hunting boots
My lover crashes through the snapping bracken.

The still gorse-hissing hill burns, brags gold broom's
Outcropping quartz; each touched bush spills dew.
Strangely last moment's parting was never sad,
But unreal like my promised years; less felt
Than this intense and silver snail calligraphy
Scrawled here in the sun across these stones.

Why have I often wanted to cry out
More against his going when he has left my flesh
Only for the night? When he has gone out
Hot from my mother's kitchen, and my combs
Were on the table under the lamp, and the wind
Was banging the doors of the shed in the yard.

Glyn Jones

Traditional Verses

16th and 17th century

A North Wales girl was once my passion,
She'd got two costumes, both in fashion,
Two matching hats as well, the peach,
And two false faces under each.

(tr. Glyn Jones)

*

I thought if only I could marry,
I'd sing and dance and live so gaily;
But all the wedded bliss I see
Is rock the cradle, hush the baby.

(tr. Gwyn Jones)

*

On the sea-shore lies a boulder
Where I loitered with my lover.
There, where wet sea winds are blowing
Thyme and rosemary are growing.

(tr. Siân James)

*

Place your hand, before you leave me
Neath my breast, and then, believe me,
You shall hear, this trouble taking,
A little sound of something breaking.

(tr. Siân James)

When we two Walked

When we two walked in Lent
We imagined that happiness
Was something different
And this was something less.

But happy were we to hide
Our happiness, not as they were
Who acted in their pride
Juno and Jupiter:

For the Gods in their jealousy
Murdered that wife and man,
And we that were wise live free
To recall our happiness then.

Edward Thomas

Stateless

In some nissen-hut of my mind
I have a stacked bed-roll, wooden chair,
suitcase plastered with peeling labels,
and a cheap clock measuring lethargic days.
I have no papers. Sometimes I am offered
forged ones, at too high a price.
Now you come, promising real
identity cards. Forgive me if till they arrive
I think it too early to rejoice.

Ruth Bidgood

from: *Jehoidah's Gents*

'My old woman,' the foreman raged in Central Cleansing. 'My old woman this, my old woman that...' The foreman liked his few jars and after a good Sunday wet, he would smack his lips appreciatively and boastfully inform the boys that he was always last to leave the Club, and no one would dare say a word when he got home. The boys said his dinner was always fried to a crisp and he was only allowed out on condition he washed every dish in the house the moment he arrived back, but it made no difference. It was such 'an old woman that Jehoidah wished for, someone to complain about, a name to drop, even disparagingly, in the company of like minded fellows.

'What d'you think my old woman put in my box today? Jam sandwiches! I'll give her what for!'

Such talk was the meat and drink of idle mornings in Central Cleansing and how Jehoidah would have loved to have joined in with the men, elbow on the counter, cap flat aback with yet another tale of 'the one I got'.

And from the first, The Vida had seemed – he had to admit it – eminently suitable for this role. Like himself, she never seemed to have been young. You could not imagine her in a pretty dress or tripping a light fantastic, and like Jehoidah, she seemed to be permanently middle-aged.

'I can take most things, boys, but the way my old woman looks at me on a Friday...'

He might, he might not, use the words, old tart.

'My old tart may be small, a little *twt*, but my God, she's got a tongue on her!'

All roads led to this image in his mind.

Alun Richards

Soap Opera

We are woken in the early hours,
our hands clearing lines of sight
through condensation in the windows.

Pulled from sleep's long downward reach
into what we dream and wish, we watch
the soap opera of a warring couple in the street –

...a drink or two... having dinner...
thought you... never wanted... fuck off home...
you come back here...

They circle in the sour pool of the street light,
and we are curtained witnesses to a moment's ugliness
all four of us will, at different speeds, forget.

Back under the duvet we brush lips goodnight
then move apart to each one's side of the bed
where dreams collide with the words unsaid.

Out on the road, beyond our gates
and high privet hedge, the taxis throttle
away out of town to the estates.

Now you shiver and curl right to the edge
– for my hand was chilled by the damp pane it wiped
to show night, sad voices, a web of uncertain light.

Tony Curtis

The Ladies of Llanbadarn

Plague take the women here –
I'm bent down with desire,
Yet not a single one
I've trysted with, or won,
Little girl, wife or crone,
Not one sweet wench my own!

What mischief is it, or spite,
That damns me in their sight?
What harm to a fine-browed maid
To have me in deep glade?
No shame for her 'twould be
In a lair of leaves to see me.

No time was, but I did love;
Never so fixed a spell did prove
That natures like old Garwy's knew –
Every day, one or two!
For all this, I can go
No nearer than a foe.
In Llanbadarn every Sunday
Was I, and (judge who may)
Towards chaste girls I faced,
My nape to a God rightly chaste,
And through my plumes gazed long
At that religious throng.
One gay bright girl says on
To t'other prudent-prospering one –

'That pale and flirt-faced lad
With hair from his sister's head –
Adulterous must be the gaze
Of a fellow with such ways.'

'Is he that sort?' demands
The girl on her right hand,
'Be damned to him, he'll stay
Unanswered till Judgement day!'

O sudden and mean reward
For dazed love the brightgirl's word!
Needs I must pack my gear,
Put paid to dreams and fear,
And manfully set out
Hermit, like rogue or lout.
But O, my glass doth show
With backward-looking woe
I'm finished, I'm too late,
Wry-necked, without a mate!

Dafydd ap Gwilym
(tr. Tony Conran)

Englyn

If you are false, as men say;
Foolish in every way,
Strange, then, that God should dare
Fashion you so fair.

Anon., 17th century
(tr. Siân James)

The Man Under the Tub

As the extravagant woman
was minding the house on her own
she saw the lad she loved most
coming in to join her,
and he threw her on the bed,
he did better than the man of the house.
And as they were lying together
under the coverlets
they did hear the husband
saying to his fellow-labourer,
'We'll go and plough the land
which is between the house and the kiln.'
The wife leapt nimbly
and shoved the man under a tub,
and she herself lay down
on the bed groaning.

'O God, what has afflicted
my darling who was fine earlier on?'

'Many an affliction, many a pain,
after toil and travail,
comes to our sex
which we dare not express.
Go and tell the woman yonder
about the sickness which afflicts me.
Say I am laid low
of the same affliction that she had last year,
and that I am in danger of death
from the affliction which she too once had.'

'Tell her to be strong
in the same way as I was.
I'll come in a moment,
and then I'll make her better.'

And as she got an opportunity
whilst the corn drier was having his dinner,
she put a fire-brand into the kiln
until it was a blazing fire.
Whilst all the neighbours
were putting out the raging fire,
the wife lifted up the tub,
the man reached the hazel grove;
the wife lost her titbit,
the man kept his life.

Anon., 15 century
(tr. Dafydd Johnston)

from: *A Heifer Without Blemish*

'Your father speaks sense, Tomos nice,' said Katto. 'It's time you wedded. Do you look round you for one like the wife of Tydu. Is she not tidy and saving? Was she not carting dung into the field when she was full? You will be five over forty in the eleventh month.'

Deio took out from his mouth the tobacco that was therein and placed it on the table, and he also emptied his mouth of its tainted spittle. 'Be you restful now, folk bach,' he said, 'for am I not going to speak about religion?' Then he raised his face and sang after the manner of the Welsh preacher: 'Me and your mam are full of years, and the hearse from Capel Sion will soon take us home to the Big Man's Palace — a home, Tomos, where we will wear White Shirts, and where there is no old rent to pay. Tomos, Tomos, weepful you will be when I am up above. Little Great One, keep an eye on Tomos. Be with your son in Capel Sion. Amen.'

When he had made an end, he put the tobacco back into his mouth, and he said: 'One hundred and half a hundred sovereigns is the mortgage on Parcdu now.'

'Do you listen, Tomos bach,' Katto counselled her son.

'Go off yourself tomorrow to the April Fair to search for a woman,' said Deio.

Tomos said: 'Iss, iss, indeed, then.'

'And take you a cask of butter with you,' said Katto. 'Leave you the butter in the back of the old trap till your eyes have fallen upon a maid; and when she has found favour with you, ask her to sell for you the butter. If she has got a sharp tongue in her mouth and makes a good bargain, say to her that you will marry her, but if she is not free of tongue, say you nothing more to her, but go in search of another.'

Deio spoke: 'Tell her your father sits in the Big Seat in Sion, in the parish of Troedfawr, in shire Cardigan. As earnest of your intention say that you are commanded to buy a heifer to start life with in Dinas. Now, little son, don't you say anything about the old mortgage.'

Tomos promised to observe his father's instructions.

'Get you there early in the morning, then,' his father said to him. 'Put the black mare in the car. And, Tomos, don't you give a ride to anybody, for fear those old robbers of excise men will catch you.'

'Make yourself comely,' said Katto. 'And when you get there, put out your belly largely. See too that you get a heifer without blemish.'

Tomos shaved his chin and his long upper lip and combed his side whiskers, and he put axle-grease on his boots, and clothed himself in his Sabbath garments of homespun cloth; and harnessing the black mare to the car, in the back of which he placed a cask full of butter, he set out for the Fair of the month of April. Tomos got out of the car at Penrhiw, as the ascent from there into Castellybryn is rocky and steep, and guided the mare by the bridle. At the foot of the hill – this morning a street of many people and much cattle – he turned into the yard of the Drivers' Arms.

'Fair morning, Tomos the son of Deio,' said the ostler of the Drivers' Arms to him.

'Say you have an empty stall, little son?' Tomos asked.

'Surely.'

'Fair morning, Tomos. How was you, man? And how was your old father?'

Tomos turned round and looked into the face of Job of the Stallion.

'Quite well, thanks be to you, Job bach.'

'What's your errand, boy bach? Old Deio your father did not say anything the day before today.'

Job, his small feet planted close together underneath his bandy legs, gazed reproachfully at Tomas.

'Well – well,' said Tomos, 'am I not selling a cask of butter, man?'

'There's excuse for you now, dear me; old Katto must be mad to send you with a cask of butter to the fair. Now, now, Tomos, do you mouth to me then your errand quick at once.'

'For what you don't know that Dinas is going, man?' replied Tomos.

'But, Tomos, why act so foolish? Was not me that told old Deio about it?'

'Of course. Father wants me to take it.'

'Little Tomos, do you speak plainly. I am not curious, but what in the name of goodness are you doing here? Be you immediate, for have I not a lot of business to do?'

'Job of the Stallion, why you are so hasty for, man? Look you, indeed, I am come for a wife.'

Job pouted his lips reprovingly, and he squeezed the large, cracked mole which was between his eyebrows with forefinger and thumb.

'I blame you, Tomos, for being so secret about your affairs. He thought.

'Dango!' he exclaimed. 'There's Nell Blaenffos. Do you know Nell, Tomos?'

'Nell Blaenffos?'

'You are as stupid as a frog, man. Blaenffos. Near Henllan. Nell the daughter of Sam.'

'Is she a tidy wench?'

'For why you make me savage, Tomos? Nell is Sam's only child. She is here with her old father paying off the last of the mortgage.'

Job shouted across the yard into the inn: 'Is Nell Blaenffos there?'

'Dammo!' came the reply. 'She was here this one minute. Nell Blaenffos! Nell Blaenffos!'

Many voices repeated the call. They cried: 'Nell Blaenffos! Nell Blaenffos! Job of the Stallion wants you.'

Caradoc Evans

Gambit

Sick of all his women
you tried to hit back with jealousy:
chose a name and a career,
researched your phantom lover

through encyclopedias,
the business pages,
fleshed him with the jargon
of import/export.

Those absent afternoons,
did you walk the shops,
kick heels from a park bench?

Those obviously-stolen evenings—
was suspicion raised by your smudged face,
the cinema's smoke in your hair?

And when he confronted you,
believed your lies of an affair,
how smug he looked, so knowing and relieved
at what he took for your guilt.

Pouring a drink, he smiled through the back of
    his hand.
Giving his nose that characteristic rub,
'Join me,' he said, 'and
welcome to the club.'

Tony Curtis

from: *Saturday Night*

When she got out of the town she felt easier. All the way along the streets, with their thin, fitful lamps alight, the whiff of the slums and 'courts' in their foul cluster; the weight of it, the sense of it, oppressed her. She felt as though she would choke, that she was too tight to breathe; her breasts rose and fell in her choler and her hands gripped and loosened themselves as she went.

But once without the town she felt better. There was a big round harvest moon that went on steadily across the sky, a ripe edge to it, and the little fleeces of cloud hung draped about like streamers. When it came right out of the cloud the valley all before her rose up out of the darkness, very gently, in a swill of light: the fields and the tall nodding elms of the Plas, and the Severn in a long white streak and the hills all around about, very quiet and still; and then there, up beyond her home, the ragged edge of mountain framed up in the sky. It was all so still and quiet, with that first autumnal breath on it – the soft, subdued light-in-darkness of the autumn. She stood there on a stile, the anger gone out of her like a puff. Anyhow it was all over.

All over – a faint fear, an unalterable little dead weight of dread, came to take possession of her. What did it matter – she did not love him, she told herself. Did she? No – how could she? But she felt sorry now – sorry for him, sorry for herself, sorry for life, sorry for everything.

Right up the valley the moonlight went, flooding it – the clear crisp fields, empty now with the harvest gathered, the brown, ripe stubble like the squares on a quilt, holding the texture; the ripe, brittle ends of a life that had gone, slowly to moulder into the earth with the rain and snow of winter. The winter was coming – but then there would be spring again soon, and then the summer and another harvest – and then winter again.

She did not love him – not really. How nice it would be – to be really in love, with somebody...

The tears were streaming down her face. She pretended not to notice them but the whole of the world before her was blurred and hidden. She rubbed her eyes and saw there, on the edge of sight, the old mountains up against the sky, very grey and ancient.

She heard her brother crying and hurried across the field to the little cottage by the level crossing. There was no other sound in the house: her father must have gone out on the spree, then – it was Saturday night. She ran breathless over the last field and let herself in. One of the children was on the stairs, his face wan and frightened.

'Our Emrys is fine and bad,' he said, trying not to cry.

'Hush. Go to bed. This min-nit!'

'Was it nice?' he said, disappearing.

'Go to bed,' she shouted as he scampered up.

She hurried up to the cot and took out the little figure swathed in flannel and pressed him to her.

'There, there,' she crooned. Her breasts filled and her voice came out warm and rich and infinitely tender.

She rocked the child backwards and forwards in her arms, humming the while.

'Our Meg!' he pleaded, reaching up his hot face. 'This wance?'

'Will you be good then?' she asked, setting him down and bending over him. 'Getting spoilt, you arr!'

'Pant Corlan,' whispered the other brother from the door.

'Will you go to bed!' she shouted. 'Playing a game you arr— the lot of you.'

'Pant Corlan,' he begged again.

'Oh dear. You arr wans. All of you,' she said. She wanted to laugh. The little one, free from the attack, was sitting up in bed again, waiting, his big round eyes winking.

'You arr bad, I must say,' she laughed. Everything was all right again now. She felt daft in the sudden rush of her joy.

The elder children had crept in from the other room and sat around her in a ring, their white anxious faces raised.

So she sang for them, as she promised, an old Welsh folk song, *Pant Corlan yr Wyn*, about the shearing, and then gave them, as a special treat, a song called *Hen Aelwyd Cymru* (The Old Welsh Hearth), her heart full to brimming. Her breasts had gone out in the flood-tide of her emotion and the old hiraeth came up in her throat; her eyes were half shut in the longing, and her beautiful contralto voice, clear and low, went out with an infinite tenderness.

'There now,' she said at last, as she sent off the elder children to their room. 'That will be three-and-sixpence if you please. Front seats!'

As she tucked up the little one for the night he said, half awake:

'Our Meg...?'

'Hush.'

'You're...not going to go away?'

'There's silly!' she whispered.

'Fine and nice,' he said, turning over drowsily, the songs still with him.

That was to be her recompense.

Geraint Goodwin

Two Letters

Alun Lewis to Freda Aykroyd, 1943

I can feel her love all the time, its reality and its deep tides...
It would be impossible for me not to love her....

The trouble is in the conflict of two tides of loving. I hoped
devoutly there need be no conflict; perhaps later there won't
be, perhaps my being will grow enough to understand the
coexistence of things: but now it's trouble in me, trouble in the
mind & in the body, and I don't know, I just don't know, darling. Do you know? Can you tell me? I'm so weary with wanting your hand & lips and aloneness. I'm so worthless, too,
beloved. You have asked me to be careful of our love. Love is
one of the few things we can't be careful about. It lives & dies
in its own nature. Care can not foster it, nor lack of care kill
it. All it asks is honesty. That is all I'm trying to give. Honesty
and love....

Freda, I'm not asking you for your advice or to do anything.
I only want you to know. If you know it will be infinitely happier for me. I can love you if you know how I am made. Perhaps there is nothing new in this to you. I think of you saying
Yes, you knew it all. Does it alter anything? Will you still
come, and will you know that the love I give you is true love?

*

The problem is so utterly simple, darling, and so utterly insoluble. I would come to you through all evil elements and death-surges; and yet I cannot come to you except when I am with you. (This isn't true.) When I am with you the problem has ceased to exist. *We are.* That is complete. At all other times this love is a cruelty to the other love I receive and have given, which so powerfully shaped and directed me that its compulsions & recollection are as normal & real as my daily answers to the daily tasks & situations in which I live in the army. You knew all this... And I would not have imagined that this also could happen which happened to us, nor that we could enter in of ourselves into such liberty and such untrammelled ways. It was bound to be restricted in many ways. The most obvious is the impediment of time...And the other obstructions lie inside us and sometimes they choke me. I've fought very hard you know, darling, since I met you, very very hard. Really fought and fought. And when it's been very hard I've made myself endure the hardness & not try to end it in some false way. And I know we need a long time for ourselves to be understood... I am not afraid of you or of me. There is only one fear in me at all. That is *for* Gweno. I love her and can hurt her too much. I would prefer to lie or die or not be born than hurt her like that. Oh Freda darling, I don't know what all this is going to become. Do you, beloved?... Don't call me conscience-ridden. There's never been guilt in us, thank God, never from the beginning of time have we – you to me & I to you – had guilt.

from: *Country Dance*

'Have you seen the Roman soldiers marching through Craig Dinas and the White Lady that drowned herself in Llyn-tro?' (The turning pool).

'Never, and I have fished it many a night alone. All I heard was an otter splashing off the bank. It's a lonely place after dark under those trees, with the water rushing over the stones. There's never hardly much of a moon down there.'

I cannot see his face, but his voice changes after a moment. He points down where we came from.

'There are no lights in Tan y Bryn, you see? Gwen Powys sits by the hearth knitting stockings in the dark to save candles, and if Megan and Margiad are not out visiting or courting, they have to go to bed. It's well for them they are handsome girls.'

'You speak discontented, Gabriel,' I says, thinking he has good reason for it.

'I have worked here fifteen years, and now I have done with Wales – done with it. Come spring we will be married. Perhaps I can find a place over the Border, where candle-ends count for less. Ah! If I can win the trials.'

He sits there silent with his arm round my waist.

'Look,' I say, 'the moon is up, we can count the sheep.'

'There's all the night before us. Now I can see you, Ann. How beautiful you are!'

He takes the pins from my hair and pulls it round my shoulders.

I struggle to be free of him, but he holds me fast.

'Light the lantern for me, Gabriel, and let me go.'

He scowls.

'You love that Welshman! Time was when you could bear to be beside me half an hour without whining to be off.'

'Time never was when I would sit on the mountain till midnight. Loose me, I tell you.'

'We are doing no wrong here together,' says Gabriel angrily.

I am affeared. Suddenly I loose his arm and run from him down the path. He comes away after me, then stays at the edge of the Basin shouting and cursing.

In my heart I know now that we shall never marry.

Margiad Evans

To Amoret

Nimble sigh, on thy warm wings,
Take this message and depart:
Tell Amoret, that smiles and sings,
At what thy airy voyage brings,
That thou cam'st lately from my heart.

Tell my lovely foe that I
Have no more such spies to send,
But one or two that I intend,
Some few minutes ere I die,
To her white bosom to commend.

Then whisper by that holy spring,
Where for her sake I would have died,
Whilst those water-nymphs did bring
Flowers to cure what she had tried;
And of my faith and love did sing.

That if my Amoret; if she
In after-times would have it read,
How her beauty murder'd me,
With all my heart I will agree,
If she'll but love me, being dead.

Henry Vaughan

from: *Rape of the Fair Country*

She was half way up the Coity before I caught her, and
turned her to my lips. Gasping, leaning upon each other, we
laughed a little and then walked on, hand in hand.

'I told him,' said she at length. 'The damned old God-bo-
therer he is, and not a streak of the Christian in him.'

'Oh, he is not so bad,' I said.

'No indeed, he is not – he is wicked. A lot of old soaking
about the benefits of Chapel over Church and then biblical
quotations and a preaching of blood and killing to make the
Devil dance. Iestyn, I am afraid.'

'Do not heed him,' I said.

'I will not,' said she. 'But will you? All the old ones are the
same now, telling the young ones to get set for the battle, but
you will not find an old one in sight when the Redcoats come
out. O, Iestyn, where will you land us if you follow the Chartists? Keep by me, boy. Leave it to the old ones.'

'To hell with the Chartists,' I said. 'Do not tell me you ran
me up here just to talk the politics.'

The leaves of past autumns were piled here, a softer bed
than made by man. Her breath was warm and sweet, and beyond the curve of her cheek I saw the mountain sweeping
away in blueness down to the red fires of the Garn. The wind
breathed about us, twanging the branches like harp strings
and hissing softly through the grass. Mari slipped to my feet
and the sight of her lying there brought the old dryness and
trembling back from the days of courting. Long and slim she
looked, a part of the dusk in her loveliness. Kneeling, I kissed
her, and she turned away her face as I unbuttoned the high
neck of her dress, and her heart throbbed wildly under my
hand.

'There is stupid,' she whispered, 'with a good strong bed
back home and sheets.'

'But beautiful, Mari. Will you have me here?'

Wildly she kissed me then and her arms went about me
hard and strong, and her hands moved over my body, making
me the loved and her the lover. The stifled sobbing of her

breath against my mouth became a whisper as she held me closer.

The moon, respectful, hid while I loved her, pulling down black dresses over her brightness, covering us with night and a temple of silence. Warm and quick was Mari beneath me, responding in wildness and a murmuring joy as I divided her body, and the lightning of youth flashed between us. And then, spent and near sleeping, we laid together, kissing, while the world of wind and water crept back with all its sounds.

Alexander Cordell

The Flirt

A pretty game, my girl,
To play with me so long;
Until this other lover
Comes dancing to thy song,
And my affair is over.

But love, though well adored,
Is not my only note:
So let thy false love-prattle
Be in another man's throat.
That weaker man's death rattle.

Ah, such as though, at last,
Will take a false man's hand:
Think kindly then of me,
When thou'rt forsaken, and
The shame sits on thy knee.

W.H. Davies

WINTER

Winter

Mountain snow, white the ravine;
By rushing wind trees are bent;
Many a couple love one another
Though they never come together.

Anon., 12th century
(tr. Tony Conran)

When all my Five and Country Senses See

When all my five and country senses see,
The fingers will forget green thumbs and mark
How, through the halfmoon's vegetable eye,
Husk of young stars and handfull zodiac,
Love in the frost is pared and wintered by,
The whispering ears will watch love drummed away
Down breeze and shell to a discordant beach,
And, lashed to syllables, the lynx tongue cry
That her fond wounds are mended bitterly.
My nostrils see her breath burn like a bush.

My one and noble heart has witnesses
In all love's countries, that will grope awake;
And when blind sleep drops on the spying senses,
The heart is sensual, though five eyes break.

Dylan Thomas

Hudson's Geese

'...I have, from time to time, related some incident of my boyhood,
and these are contained in various chapters in *The Naturalist in
La Plata, Birds and Man, Adventures among Birds...*'
      W.H. Hudson, in *Far Away and Long Ago.*

Hudson tells us of them,
the two migrating geese,
she hurt in the wing
indomitably walking
the length of a continent,
and he wheeling above,
calling his distress.
They could not have lived.
Already I see her wing
scraped past the bone
as she drags it through rubble.
A fox, maybe, took her
in his snap jaws. And what
would he do, the point
of his circling gone?
The wilderness of his cry
falling through an air
turned instantly to winter
would warn the guns of him.
If a fowler dropped him,
let it have been quick,
pellets hitting brain
and heart so his weight
came down senseless,
and nothing but his body
to enter the dog's mouth.

                    Leslie Norris

Mythologies

Because you killed the dragon named Despair

I make for you a castle out of gold
To stand beyond the plain we battled for.
You are the sun king yet we'll winter here,
Your silk light falls upon our gentle court:
Eternal summer, like Peredur's tree
Forever burning and forever green,
Your presence brings, your silver kisses seem.

And when you sleep it is an enchanted dark
Falls from your eyes and keeps us safe apart
From the owl's cry, the raven, and the wolf.
Your poet, page, my lines shall serve your fame,
Though we in time to other bodies change:

There shall be legends strewn across the plain.

John Ackerman

Anti-Clockwise

'Nothing to do with sex, doctor.' Her voice dies.
In the consulting room's firegrate, no fire.
Last summer's dried flowers, sweet lies, nest there.

Now if through her eyes I could slowly pan,
with ophthalmoscope, would I blunderingly
light up single beds in separate bedrooms?

Whispers and sighs. I cannot say, 'What?' again.
So observe her mouth's theatre, how she turns
and turns her wedding ring, anti-clockwise.

Dannie Abse

133

Snap at Cold Knap 1938

The face I remember, and the name Vanessa.
Even through this mist she looks a rebel dresser.

Spain was a distant Bren-gun spit, young Auden unread.
We would cycle from the city with kissing ahead.

Kissing was the most that we dared do then.
The damp hulk of Bethesda loomed over her men.

We bounded to the sea in respectable rig.
But beneath my flannel the enemy was big.

Those days in heat like a mongrel dog
Panted to a close like some marathon slog.

She married into timber, Rolls at the door,
But the itch soon told her what lay in store.

Now she is split from her partner and brood,
The gin's tilted back, all her lovers are crude.

John Tripp

Like That

He remembers how younger,
when he was reading about love,
his love would come quietly
to his room to challenge
description, and how he would put
the book down and listen to her
version of it, with rain
falling, perhaps, and the wind loud.

Selah! It is now he who must
go, and from the familiar prose
of her body make his way back
to his book, to the memory
rather of those earlier evenings, when
too willingly he laid it aside.

R.S. Thomas

Contact

She came up to him at closing time
among the hulks of breath outside the Cock,
hugging herself, too late
for the preliminary swift half
well understood among plenty.
'Where d'youse stay?' she said.

He muttered something polite
and disappointing: he could have reached out
and touched her, but he had somewhere to go.
She thanked him, calling him 'mister'
in a way that jarred him out of indifference.
She turned back to the mouth of the Underground.

Neither of them streetwise or proverbial-sly
she was trying this for the first time
and there was still some diffident fantasy
of spontaneous choice, that evaporated
when she thought of waking
to the colourless surprise of a man's back,

shelter meaning much until you have it
like a complicated dream of hunger:
bald towels hung at the bathroom door
like a pair of admonitory crows.
He could hear the rain in the sodden hills
around her shoulders, see the hidden scars

flower to open the contours of irony on her lips,
curling hard among the country syllables.
Like hunks of white bread drifting in pale ale
there were manly expectations in the air:
the best lacked all conviction,
and she knew where to find the rougher trade.

Asleep in their separate lives,
there was an inky silence over the water
but just below, small crustaceans
were busy with secrets and pincers,

using their shells to build settlements,
timescales, lessons and islands
eating all the while in minuscule detail.

Bees came and went on the sea
and they both swam in the whisper,
which in her dream became her father's shout.

Steve Griffiths

136

Dyddgu Replies to Dafydd

All year in open places, underneath
   the frescoed forest ceiling,
   we have made ceremony
   out of this seasonal love.

Dividing the leaf-shade as divers white
   in green pools we rose to dry
   islands of sudden sun. Then
   love seemed generosity.

Original sin I whitened from your
   mind, my colours influenced
   your flesh, as sun on the floor
   and warm furniture of a church.

So did our season bloom in mild weather,
   reflected gold like butter
   under chins, repeatedly
   unfolding to its clock of seed.

Autumn, our forest room is growing cold.
   I wait, shivering, feeling a
   dropping sun, a coming dark,
   your heart changing the subject.

The season coughs as it falls, like a coal;
   the trees ache. The forest falls
   to ruin, a roofless minster
   where only two still worship.

Love still, like sun, a vestment, celebrates,
   its warmth about our shoulders.
   I dread the day when Dyddgu's once
   loved name becomes a common cloak.

Your touch is not so light. I grow heavy.
   I wait too long, grow anxious,
   note your changing gestures, fear
   desire's alteration.

The winter stars are flying and the owls
   sing. You are packing your songs
   in a sack, narrowing your
   words, as you stare at the road.

The feet of young men beat, somewhere far off
   on the mountain. I would women
   had roads to tread in winter
   and other lovers waiting.

A raging rose all summer falls to snow,
   keeping its continuance in
   frozen soil. I must be patient
   for the breaking of the crust.

I must be patient that you will return
   when the wind whitens the tender
   underbelly of the March grass
   thick as pillows under the oaks.

Gillian Clarke

Dyddgu is the woman to whom the medieval Welsh poet,
Dafydd ap Gwilym, addressed many of his love poems.

These Bones

What shall we be, sweet, you and I,
When the flesh that clothed us is all laid by?

Desire must end when the blood grows chill,
Love and shame and the wayward will.

No joy of touch nor of sight again:
When the nerves have rotted there's no more pain.

No dream can stir, no sweet song rise
In a gaping skull with sightless eyes.

Of all that in you is now my pride
The white teeth only will then abide.

Naught of us when life is done
But bone and bone by speechless bone;

Mute heaps, under the laughing sky,
In fleshless slumber we two shall lie.

Bones only we are – yes, laugh, sweet face,
Till the white teeth flash from their lurking place;

Laugh loud and long; but, the laughter o'er,
Bones only you'll be for evermore,

Bones on bones, my beautiful maid,
And kite and raven about your head;

And none to ask of the flying year,
'Where is the flesh that rioted here?'

T.H. Parry Williams
(tr. Idris Bell)

In Memoriam

She was my nest, she was my heaven,
A refuge for body and soul.
Her comfort she gave me,
Gave me, freely, herself.
For that time, my muse became
A bird, above earth's thorns.
Her gaze was the sun, her step the breeze,
Happiness encompassed us.
Oh my brave girl, oh golden hair,
Forever my home, my heaven.

Waldo Williams
(tr. Siân James)

Traditional Verse

Naught between us two this day
Only coffin, shroud and clay.
We've been further, far, apart,
Never with a heavier heart.

Anon., 16th – 17th century
(tr. Siân James)

from: *Smile Please*

(her autobiography)

When my first love affair came to an end I wrote this poem:

> I didn't know
> I didn't know
> I didn't know.

Then I settled down to be miserable

Jean Rhys

from: *Voyage in the Dark*

The taxi stopped and I got down and paid the man and went into the hotel.

He was waiting for me.

I smiled and said, 'Hullo.'

He had been looking very solemn but when I smiled like that he seemed relieved.

We went and sat in the corner.

I said, 'I'll have coffee.'

I imagined myself saying very calmly, 'The thing is that you don't understand. You think I want more than I do. I only want to see you sometimes, but if I never see you again I'll die. I'm dying now really, and I'm too young to die.'

...The candles crying wax tears and the smell of stephanotis and I had to go to the funeral in a white dress and a wreath round my head and the wreath in my hands made my gloves wet – they said so young to die...

The people there were like upholstered ghosts.

Jean Rhys

Owl

Cariad, since you packed
your bags, said goodbye,
my sleep's been troubled
by a hooting owl; daylong
he roosts in the rafters
of this ramshackle house,
no bother to me much, but
makes his perch at night
upon my sill, keeping me
awake until it's dawn.

I have tried many ways
to rid me of this bird:
stood at the window, shone
a lamp, clapped my hands,
but he's not to be shood.
I lie upon our bed, watch
the beaked minutes pass,
shut the curtains, walk
from room to hooting room
until the welcome light.

Cariad, since you went
beyond my love's borders,
an owl troubles my sleep.

Meic Stephens

Painting Him Out

That morning she drew back the curtains
on the promise of sun.
Now she would do it.
The brush nuzzled into the creamy tin.
Starting at the top left-hand corner
she spread the colour
so it licked over and in
to the skin of the paper,
salving the scuffs and fadings,
soothing the bruised angles and corners.
Though at each finishing stroke
the bristles razored the edged crack
between paper and wood, the hairs growing spiked
and stubborn as his with sweat after running
or love. The handle moistening in her hand,
she worked with a rhythm, giving
herself to each wall in turn,
three times until it was done.

The chair she stood upon is starred by flecks
and the whorls of her finger-prints.
The old sheets rolled away, the brush
loosening its load and softening under the tap water.
She climbs the stairs again and the sun
which had risen behind her back,
through the day lighting over her shoulder
her work, has fallen to the gable-end
and now side-lights the view from her french-windows,
applying a wash over the town, the pink-brown sea,
across to a muted, distant coastline
where, she knows, he will be
driving, or eating, or laughing
in different colours.

Tony Curtis

143

The Ruin

Nothing but a hovel now
Between moorland and meadow,
Once the owners saw in you
A comely cottage, bright, new,
Now roof, rafters, ridge-pole, all
Broken down by a broken wall.

A day of delight was once there
For me, long ago, no care
When I had a glimpse of her
Fair in an ingle-corner.
Beside each other we lay
In the delight of that day.

Her forearm, snowflake-lovely,
Softly white, pillowing me,
Proffered a pleasant pattern
For me to give in my turn,
And that was our blessing for
The new-cut lintel and door.

Now the wild wind, wailing by,
Crashes with curse and with cry
Against my stones, a tempest
Born and bred in the East,
Or south ram-batterers break
The shelter that folk forsake.

Life is illusion and grief;
A tile whirls off, as a leaf
Or a lath goes sailing, high
In the keening of kite-kill cry.
Could it be, our couch once stood
Sturdily under that wood?
Pillar and post, it would seem
Now you are less than a dream.

Are you that, or only the lost
Wreck of a riddle, rune-ghost?

'Dafydd, the cross on their graves
Marks what little it saves,
Says, *They did well in their lives.*'

Dafydd ap Gwilym
(tr. Rolfe Humphries)

Laughter Tangled in Thorn

Dressed like a child
for our ritual Sunday afternoon
pilgrimage to the hillside:
your pear-shaped hood,
scarf wound like a snake
and red ski-boots dragged along
like grown-up things worn for a dare.

When I laugh, I don't mean it to hurt.
It is the brother of the laugh
at the end of our love-making –
rigid bones melting into blood.

The moor grass has turned
into a frosty yellow, its green
gone deep into hibernation.
We crunch mud, step streams,
in games which strip us of years
like the trees have been
of their leaves. The water
and your green eyes
share the only motion.

You see a red berry
and call it a ladybird.

I think of your city upbringing;
the seasons being passing strangers
through Belfast streets
where you cadged rides from the ice.

When the brook's chatter is snow-fed,
your laughter is tangled in thorn.
You discover an ice sculpture
mounted on a spine of reed,
and call it 'Teeth and Jaws'.
The light of your words
travels through it.

High above Merthyr, mountain lapping mountain.
You are amazed at the rarified sunlight!
When you speak, the numb streets
are startled. We leave the childhood
of the moorland, to grow taller
with a tiredness which is the sister
of when we lie, translucent and still,
on the single spine of our bed.

Mike Jenkins

Madrigal

Your love is dead, lady, your love is dead,
Dribbles no sound
From his stopped lips, though swift underground
Spurts his wild hair.

Your love is dead, lady, your love is dead;
Faithless he lies.
Deaf to your call, though shades of his eyes
Break through and stare.

R.S. Thomas

from: *Acting Captain*

He sat on the edge of the sofa and put his hand idly on her moist tangled hair. 'I don't know what to do. Curly said for to take you to the hospital. I think I'd better, too. Shall I carry you tonight?'

'No,' she said, frightened. 'You can't now. It's blackout and there's bombs again, and I doubt there won't be a bed there. And you got to pay, too.' She pushed her bony hand slowly across the soiled sheet and touched his battledress. 'I don't want to go there,' she said.

She was too weak to wipe the tears out of her eyes.

'Oh Jesu!' he said, getting up in a temper. 'Don't cry then. I was only suggestin'. Do as you like. Wait till tomorrow if you like. Only I was thinking the redcaps will be coming round to look for me tomorrow.'

'Never mind about tomorrow,' she said.

'The cat's been pissing in the room somewhere,' he said, sniffing about him. He sat down again and wiped her eyes with the sheet.

'You got to mind about tomorrow,' he said.

'Remember you was jealous of me in a dance at the Mackworth when we was courting?' she said. 'You took me out and slapped me in the face, remember?'

'What about it?' he asked slowly, nonplussed.

'Slap me now, again,' she said.

He laughed.

'I'm not jealous of you no more,' he said. 'You get better, and then p'raps I'll get jealous again, see?'

She smiled and let her neck relax on the cushion.

'You'll never be jealous of me again,' she said, looking at him with her faraway eyes.

Her soul was in her eyes, and it wasn't sick like her body.

Alun Lewis

from: *The Mabinogion*

And then once upon a time Lleu went to Caer Dathyl to visit Math son of Mathonwy. The day he went to Caer Dathyl, she was stirring about the court. And she heard the blast of a horn, and after the blast of the horn, lo, a spent stag going by, and dogs and huntsmen after it, and after the dogs and the huntsmen a troop of men on foot coming. 'Send a lad,' said she,'to learn what the company is.' The lad went and asked who they were. 'This is Gronw Bebyr, he who is lord of Penllyn,' said they. And that the lad told her.

He went after the stag, and on Cynfael river he overtook the stag and slew it. And what with slaying the stag and baiting his dogs, he was busied till the night closed in on him. And as day declined and night was drawing near, he came past the gate of the court. 'Faith,' said she, 'we shall be ill-spoken of by the chieftain for letting him go at this hour to another domain, if we do not ask him in,' 'Faith, lady,' said they, 'it is only right to ask him in.' Then messengers went to meet him and ask him in. And then he accepted the invitation gladly and came to the court, and she came herself to meet him, to make him welcome, and to give him greeting. 'Lady,' said he, 'God repay thee thy welcome.'

They changed their garb and went to sit down. Blodeu-wedd looked on him, and the moment she looked there was no part of her that was not filled with love of him. And he too gazed on her, and the same thought came to him as had come to her. He might not conceal that he loved her, and he told her so. She knew great joy at heart, and their talk that night was of the affection and love they had conceived one for the other. Nor did they delay longer than that night ere they embraced each other. And that night they slept together.

And on the morrow he sought to depart. 'Faith,' said she, 'thou wilt not go from me to-night.' That night too they were together. And that night they took counsel how they might stay together. 'There is no counsel for thee,' said he,'save one:

to seek to learn from him how his death may come about, and
that under pretence of loving care for him.'

Anon., 11th century
(tr. Gwyn Jones and Thomas Jones)

Perhaps

Perhaps, he said, it will be different in
another life. We will meet,
and recognise each other instantly,
and sing quite openly the songs
we keep now in our poor, divided hearts.

And folk will smile and say yes, they are lovers,
and wish us well, and ask us to their house,
and give us wedding presents by the dozen,
and scatter us with bawdy jokes and rice.

And we will live together like the wind
lives with the rain, like butter lives with bread,
like summer lives with holidays and seas
live with the restless longing of their tides.

She listened, and she smiled, and said perhaps
when next we live you'll be the single one,
and I the one with half a dozen kids.

Herbert Williams

Portrait of a Marriage

To the suburban house you return again
with a new hat and the stammering discourse
of mild rebellion. You dare not entertain
questions like – Can I start again? Seek divorce?
Because now, middle-aged, you would gain
nothing but insecurity and remorse,
all the might-have-beens crying in the brain.

It was false even before the first caress
but how you strove to make it true,
fouling silence, talking louder to suppress
the lie that somehow grew and grew,
as you hid each new distress
behind the photograph of the smile and you
less than radiant in your wedding dress.

And, in the stabbed evenings, when the sun
died, by appointment, in its Joseph's coat,
you asked help from that anyone
whose million edition pen could write
romantic novels to overcome
the truth of the lonely all about,
the taste of nothing on your tongue.

Now, one year's gone since your clumsy honeymoon
and he talks to you behind an unlocked door;
again your artificial smile alone
floats between the ceiling and the floor,
like some quiet heartbreak, almost to condone
what, after all, others too must slow endure,
the clock, the unhappiness, the civilized bore.

Until those untamed voices in this tidy room
weirdly rise again to show
what is you and your husband's doom,

the dullness you should never know,
the silent piano in the gloom,
the cut-glass vases you endow
with flowers, to disguise this here and now.

Dannie Abse

from: *Under Mynydd Bach*

Soft days after snow,
        snowdrops
under sycamores beside the stream,
earth brown and crumbling.

Now the dark gleams softly
under catkins and water below,
alight in the February sun.
And I who desired
        eyes washed clean
as melting snow,
radiant at the point of fall,
know that every word obscures
the one I want to know.

Now soft days bear us
who take each other's hands,
and on their surface
        colder than blood
our brief appearances.

Though snowdrops follow the snow,
        and the water burns,
darkness carries them.

Our faces are taken away.

Where do you go,
        unspeakable love?

Jeremy Hooker

from: *Shacki Thomas*

'How's the missis, Shacki?'

'Thass what I going to see, chaps. Fine I do hope, ay.'

They all hoped so, and confessed as much. But they were all fools, and the worm fear was at Shacki's heart like a maggot in a swede. 'I got to go this afternoon, see,' he said, hoping for a chorus of reassurance and brave words, but– 'I remember' – Tommy Sayce took up the tale – 'When little Sammy Jones had his leg took off at the hip."'How do a chap with only one peg on him get about, doctor?" he asks old Dr Combes. "Why, mun," doctor tells him, "we'll get you a nice wooden leg, Sammy" "Ay, but will I be safe with him, doctor?" asks Sammy. "Safe? Good God, mun, you'll be timber right to the face!" Thass what doctor told him.'

'Ah, they'm marvellous places, them hospitals,' Shacki assured them, to assure himself at the same time. 'Look at the good they do do.'

'Ay, and look at the good they don't do. Didn't they let Johnny James's mam out 'cos she had cancer and they was too dull to cure it? And Johnny thinking she was better – the devils!'

The worm went ahead with his tunnelling. 'I carn stop anyway,' said Shacki, and low-spiritedly he left them to their talk. Not fifty yards away he cursed them bitterly. Death, death, death, cancer, cancer, cancer – by God, he'd like to see that big-nosed bastard Ianto Evans on his back there, and that brother of his, and Tommy Sayce, and every other knackerpant as hadn't had more feeling than a tram of rippings. Nobody have pain or everybody – that was the thing. He cleared his throat savagely and spat into the gutter as though between the eyes of the world. Self-pity for his loneliness brought too big a lump to his throat before he could curse again, and then once more it was all Gwenny fach, oh, Gwenny fach; he'd like to tear the sky in pieces to get her home again. If only she was better, if only she was home, he'd do the washing, he'd blacklead the grate, he'd scrub through every day.

Then he went into the greengrocer's, where the air smelled so much a pound. 'Nice bunch of chrysanths,' he was offered, but they were white and he rejected them. 'I ain't enamelled of them white ones. Something with a bit of colour, look.'

Gwyn Jones

Rushes of Life to the Head

Sometimes he comes through the house, calling me
And seems obsessed with finding me.

I answer – like a flute? But my voice is old.
Suddenly it is night.

I live such moments as though I had long red hair,
Eyes of hyacinth –
As though the trees of the world
Shook out new leaves, the day before felling.

Do not laugh at us –

We give each other this
Not as we are but as we were once.

Who now remembers us?

In that long room, the vases are full of silence.

Jean Earle

Breaking Surface

Out of the oiled water
weeks later, they hoisted you, lovers
married in the cold depths of the docks.
And until the dredger's knock
and buckle against your car's roof,
they'd fictioned your runaway.
A sinful flight, snatched love in rented rooms,
incognito, with the scant luggage of a shame
friends and family presumed,
the strange newnesses they'd envied.
The loved, abandoned children calling your name.

Questions rise,
bubble and break the surface:
how was the bond made?
And where? Why
into the docks, such
grim and botched waters?
And what words, sucked
from the last air
before the rush of dark.
Such probings, metallic and cold.
Cold the kiss, the deepening cries.

Our comings and goings, trade
on the slop of water, wash over,
tread down such detritus as you.
The Sunday boys cast their bait
across the length of afternoon.
The weights find bottom and anchor.
Their lines crease the slick.

Nothing pulls.
No sounds but the slapping sound
of stale trapped water.
Maybe drowned is best left drowned.

Tony Curtis

4 a.m.

The light that creeps into this room
is white as candlewax and cold.
It coats the sleeping shapes of things;
no sane sister of the dark
crawling in with its smell of wet fur
or old albino moss. Everything
hushes; breath, even, slides gentler.

If this light that seeps through crack and curtain
were gas or radiation dust
they could not lie more tidily
man and wife so carefully apart
though flexed to face the same wind's quarter.
Their faces glimmer like cooled fat.
Each suspects the other is awake.

Nearby, still whole as flowers,
their children – boy who steers a ship of light
from star to star, girl with pale hair fanned
across her pillow like a princess in a story –
defined again to daytime selves.
The shadows and the sweetnesses of dream
rubbed smooth, almost, as alabaster.

Dawn is a tundra border crossed
helplessly, as on a train. Grey shapes
of the possible block in round us.
It must be luxury to sleep right through:
to wake and, stretching, know you have,
you are.

Christine Evans

from: *Under Milk Wood*

Rosie Probert and Captain Cat

First Voice

Captain Cat, at his window thrown wide to the sun and the clippered seas he sailed long ago when his eyes were blue and bright, slumbers and voyages; ear-ringed and rolling, I love You Rosie Probert tattooed on his belly, he brawls with broken bottles in the fug and babel of the dark dock bars, roves with a herd of short and good time cows in every naughty port and twines and souses with the drowned and blowzy-breasted dead. He weeps as he sleeps and sails.

Second Voice

Once voice of all he remembers most dearly as his dream buckets down. Lazy early Rosie with the flaxen thatch, whom he shared with Tom-Fred the donkeyman and many another seaman, clearly and near to him speaks from the bedroom of her dust. In that gulf and heaven of the night; but she speaks to Captain napping Cat alone. Mrs Probert...

Rosie Probert

from Duck Lane, Jack. Quack twice and ask for Rosie

Second Voice

...is the one love of his sea-life that was sardined with women.

Rosie Probert (Softly)

What seas did you see,
Tom Cat, Tom Cat,

In your sailoring days
Long long ago?
What sea beasts were
In the wavery green
When you were my master?

Captain Cat

I'll tell you the truth.
Seas barking like seals,
Blue seas and green,
Seas covered with eels
And mermen and whales.

Rosie Probert

What seas did you sail
Old whaler when
On the blubbery waves
Between Frisco and Wales
You were my bosun?

Captain Cat

As true as I'm here
Dear you Tom Cat's tart
You landlubber Rosie
You cosy love
My easy as easy
My true sweetheart,
Seas green as a bean
Seas gliding with swans
In the seal-barking moon.

Rosie Probert

What seas were rocking
My little deck hand

My favourite husband
In your seaboots and hunger
My duck my whaler
My honey my daddy
My pretty sugar sailor
With my name on your belly
When you were a boy
Long long ago?

Captain Cat

I'll tell you no lies,
The only sea I saw
Was the seesaw sea
With you riding on it.
Lie down, lie easy.
Let me shipwreck in your thighs.

Rosie Probert

Knock twice, Jack,
At the door of my grave
And ask for Rosie.

Captain Cat

Rosie Probert.
Remember her.
She is forgetting.
The earth which filled her mouth
Is vanishing from her.
Remember me
I have forgotten you.
I am going into the darkness of the
    darkness for ever.
I have forgotten that I was ever born.

Dylan Thomas

Post-script: for Gweno

If I should go away,
Beloved, do not say
'He has forgotten me.'
For you abide,
A singing rib within my dreaming side;
You always stay.
And in the mad, tormented valley
Where blood and hunger rally
And Death the wild beast is uncaught, untamed,
Our soul withstands the terror
And has its quiet honour
Among the glittering stars your voices named.

Alun Lewis

Turning Away

I turn away and say 'You do not love me';
Cry bitterly; remember, at this tune,
How all the clichés seemed as sound as apples,
How all the days were stopped at one high noon.

Not quite believing, now I rack each sentence
For meanings that no words could ever hold;
Drag out distinctions, hesitations, use them
On either side according to the mood.

So long without you, that the summer garden
Is overgrown with weeds, a hectic crop
Whose woody stems and vast flamboyant flowers
Blot out the seedling beds they overtop.

Until at last I take them as the pattern,
Expect the skies will suddenly explode
With all the dreams at once, in technicolour,
No effort now, no diffidence allowed.

And when that does not happen, and the poppies
Wither in sudden dryness, overlook
The slow, established colour of the garden,
Rose tree, forget-me-not and seedling oak:

But turn away and say 'You do not love me';
Of all the clichés note but only this,
Most lovers die, incur their final glory
Only through pain; that love's translated loss.

Sally Roberts Jones

Goodbye

So we must say Goodbye, my darling,
And go, as lovers go, for ever;
Tonight remains, to pack and fix on labels
And make an end of lying down together.

I put a final shilling in the gas,
And watch you slip your dress below your knees
And lie so still I hear your rustling comb
Modulate the autumn in the trees.

And all the countless things I shall remember
Lay mummy-cloths of silence round my head;
I fill the carafe with a drink of water;
You say 'We paid a guinea for this bed,'

And then, 'We'll leave some gas, a little warmth
For the next resident, and these dry flowers,'
And turn your face away, afraid to speak
The big word, that Eternity is ours.

Your kisses close my eyes and yet you stare
As though God struck a child with nameless fears;
Perhaps the water glitters and discloses
Time's chalice and its limpid useless tears.

Everything we renounce except our selves;
Selfishness is the last of all to go;
Our sighs are exhalations of the earth,
Our footprints leave a track across the snow.

We made the universe to be our home,
Our nostrils took the wind to be our breath,
Our hearts are massive towers of delight,
We stride across the seven seas of death.

Yet when all's done you'll keep the emerald
I placed upon your finger in the street;
And I will keep the patches that you sewed
On my old battledress tonight, my sweet.

Alun Lewis

Like the Touch of Rain

Like the touch of rain she was
On a man's flesh and hair and eyes
When the joy of walking thus
Has taken him by surprise:

With the love of the storm he burns,
He sings, he laughs, well I know how,
But forgets when he returns
As I shall not forget her 'Go now.'

Those two words shut a door
Between me and the blessed rain
That was never shut before
And will not open again.

Edward Thomas

A Letter

Alun Lewis to Freda Aykroyd, 1943

I've been indifferent to love this week, it began on Sunday afternoon. I could even tell you about that. I've been working pretty well all day for the last week & I haven't had any time to consider my self except when I stole two hours on Sunday afternoon. I went down to the lake and swam. On the way down through the long cotton grass whose ears are thorny parachutes that prick your ankles as you walk I aided three Indian boys in chasing an iguana. It was a beautiful beast. They had cornered it in a currant bush & I saw it break cover & I shouted & pointed to the swaying line of grass and they chased it and stoned it and killed it. It was like killing Lawrence's snake. An obscenity. My only motive in disclosing its escape was to know what beast it was. It was a beautiful huge three foot lizard, a soft sleek brown. Its body was very tranquil in death. They cut off its tail, which has an aphrodisiac secretion in a gland. I went on then to the lake where I was quite alone & stripped by the brown flood water under the bushes and let the sun smooth my body & my genitals. And my body was thinking of you & me. But my mind said very remotely, like an arbiter, 'Body is captivated, but the mind is not at one with the body.' And at that antilogy the body withdrew its thoughts & the desire as if rebuked & I went & swam my body and came back wet & fishlike & insentient. You were NOT there; and my mind said it so implacably: the world has harsh and final demands which I must fulfil. The rest is not possible until the demands of the world are admitted & executed. I hate this passionately, passionately, passionately.

Talysarn

Bone-aged is my white horse;
Blunted is the share;
Broken the man who through sad land
Broods on the plough.

Bone-bright was my gelding once;
Burnished was the blade;
Beautiful the youth who in green Spring
Broke earth with song.

Brenda Chamberlain

Strays

Of all the women of the fields –
    full skirt, small waist –
the scarecrow is the best dressed.

She has an air about her
    which more than makes up
for her loss of face.

There is nothing between us.
    If I take her arm
there is nowhere to go.

We are alone and strollers
    of a fine day with
under us the earth's fathoms waiting.

R.S. Thomas

Last Words

Splendidly, Shakespeare's heroes,
Shakespeare's heroines, once the spotlight's on
enact every night, with such grace, their verbose deaths.
Then great plush curtains, then smiling resurrection
to applause – and never their good looks gone.

The last recorded words too
of real kings, real queens, all the famous dead,
are but pithy pretences, quotable fictions
composed by anonymous men decades later,
never with ready notebooks at the bed.

Most do not know who they are
when they die or where they are, country or town,
nor which hand on their brow. Some clapped out actor may
imagine distant clapping, bow, but no real queen
will sigh, 'Give me my robe, put on my crown.'

Death scenes not life-enhancing,
death scenes not beautiful nor with breeding;
yet bravo Sidney Carton, bravo Duc de Chavost
who euphoric, beside the guillotine, turned down
the corner of the page he was reading.

And how would I wish to go?
Not as in opera – that would offend –
nor like a blue-eyed cowboy shot and short of words,
but finger-tapping still our private morse, '...love you,'
before the last flowers and flies descend.

Dannie Abse

Great Nights Returning

Great nights returning, midnight's constellations
Gather from groundfrost that unnatural brilliance.
Night now transfigures, walking in the starred ways,
Tears for the living.

Earth now takes back the secret of her changes.
All the wood's dropped leaves listen to your footfall.
Night has no tears, no sound among the branches;
Stopped is the swift stream.

Spirits were joined when hazel leaves were falling.
Then the stream hurrying told of separation.
This is the fires' world, and the voice of Autumn
Stilled by the death-wand.

Under your heels the icy breath of Winter
Hardens all roots. The Leonids are flying.
Now the crisp stars, the circle of beginning;
Death, birth, united.

Nothing declines here. Energy is fire-born.
Twigs catch like stars or serve for your divining.
Lean down and hear the subterranean water
Crossed by the quick dead.

Now the soul knows the fire that first composed it
Sinks not with time but is renewed hereafter.
Death cannot steal the light which love has kindled
Nor the years change it.

Vernon Watkins

ACKNOWLEDGEMENTS

We would like to thank the following authors, owners of copyright, publishers, literary agents and executors for permission to reprint the poems and extracts of prose printed in this anthology.

Dannie Abse and Sheil Land Associates for 'Epithalamion', 'Portrait of a Marriage', and 'Last Words' from *White Coat, Purple Coat: Collected Poems* (Hutchinson, 1989); 'Anti-Clockwise' from *Remembrance of Crimes Past* (Hutchinson, 1990); and the extract from *Ash on a Young Man's Sleeve* (Penguin, 1989).

John Ackerman for 'Mythologies' from *The Image and the Dark* (Gomer, 1975).

Graham Allen for 'The Song she Brought' first published in *Poetry Wales*, Spring 1979, vol. 14, No.4.

Freda Aykroyd for four letters to her from Alun Lewis, written in 1943.

Ruth Bidgood for 'Swallows' and 'Stateless' from *Not Without Homage* (Christopher Davies, 1975).

Michael Burn for 'Welsh Love Letter' from *Open Day & Night* (Chatto & Windus, 1978).

Gillian Clarke for 'Choughs', 'Sailing', and 'Dyddgu Replies to Dafydd', all originally published in *Poetry Wales*. Reprinted in *The Sundial* (Gomer, 1978). 'Choughs' and 'Dyddgu...' also printed in her *Selected Poems* (Carcanet, 1985).

Joseph Clancy for his translation 'A Pregnant Woman' by Bobi Jones from *Bobi Jones: Selected Poems* (Christopher Davies, 1987).

Tony Conran for his translations of 'The North Star' by John Morris-Jones, 'The Shirt of a Lad' (Anon.), 'Glint' by Euros Bowen, 'The Ladies of Llanbadarn' by Dafydd ap Gwilym, 'Winter' (Anon.), and 'Gwalchmai's Boast' by Gwalchmai ap Meilyr, all from his *Welsh Verse* (Poetry Wales Press, 1986).

David Higham Associates for the Estate of Alexander Cordell for the extract from *Rape of the Fair Country* (Victor Gollancz, 1959).

Tony Curtis for 'Letter from John', 'Gambit', and 'Field of Wheat' from his *Selected Poems* (Seren, 1986), 'Soap Opera' as published in *The Cambridge Review*, 'Painting Him Out', and 'Breaking Surface' from *The Last Candles* (Seren, 1989).

Gomer Press for the Estate of Idris Davies for 'Put your Arms Around my Body' and 'Let's go to Barry Island...' from his *Collected Poems* (Gomer, 1972).

Jean Earle for 'Rushes of Life to the Head' from *Visiting Light* (Poetry Wales Press, 1987).

Jane Edwards and D. Llwyd Morgan for his translation of the extract from 'Blind Date' by Jane Edwards from *The Penguin Book of Welsh Short Stories* edited by Alun Richards (Penguin, 1976).

John Harris for the Estate of Caradoc Evans for permission to print an extract of 'A Heifer Without Blemish' from *My People* (Andrew Melrose, 1915), reprinted (Seren, 1987).

Christine Evans for '4 a.m.' from *Cometary Phases* (Seren,1989).

Cassandra Davies for the Estate of Margiad Evans for permission to reprint extracts from *Country Dance*.

Myfanwy Lumsden for the Estate of Geraint Goodwin for permission to reprint the extract from 'Saturday Night' from *The Collected Stories of Geraint Goodwin* (H.G. Walters, 1976).

Steve Griffiths for 'News of a Marriage' from *Civilised Airs* (Poetry Wales Press,1984) and 'Contact' from *Uncontrollable Fields* (Seren,1990). 'News of a Marriage' originally published in the magazine *Element 5* in 1983.

Jeremy Hooker for 'Under Mynydd Bach' from *Englishman's Road* (Carcanet, 1980) and *A View from the Source: Selected Poems* (Carcanet, 1982).

Emyr Humphreys for the extract from 'Mel's Secret Love' from *Natives* (Secker & Warburg, 1968). Reprinted in *The Penguin Book of Welsh Short Stories*, 1976.

Rolfe Humphries for his translations of 'In Morfudd's Arms' and 'The Ruin' by Dafydd ap Gwilym from *The Oxford Book of Welsh Verse in English* (Oxford University Press, 1973), originally published in *Nine Thorny Thickets: Selected Poems of Dafydd ap Gwilym* (Kent State University Press, 1969).

Janet Jackson for the Estate of Kenneth Hurlstone Jackson for his translation of the sixteenth century anonymous poem 'He Whose Hand and Eye are Gentle' from his *Celtic Miscellany* (Penguin, 1971).

Siân James for permission to reprint an extract from *Dragons & Roses* (Duckworth, 1983) and for her translations of anonymous englynion, Traditional Verses, and 'In Memoriam' by Waldo Williams.

Mike Jenkins for 'Laughter Tangled in Thorn' from *Empire of Smoke*, (Poetry Wales Press, 1983).

Nigel Jenkins for 'Shirts', originally published in *Poetry Wales*, but widely anthologised and included in his *Acts of Union: Selected Poems* (Gomer, 1990).

Dafydd Johnston for his translations of 'Bundling', 'The Man in the Tub', and 'Englyn to the Penis' from his *Medieval Welsh Erotic Love Poems* (TAFOL, 1991).

R. Gerallt Jones for his translation of 'Violet' by Bryan Martin Davies from *Poems of Wales 1930-1970* (Gomer, 1974).

Glyn Jones for permission to reprint an extract from 'The Saviour' originally from *The Water Music* (Routledge, 1944), reprinted in *Selected Short Stories* (Dent, 1971); for 'Esyllt' from *Poems* (Fortune Press, 1939) and *Selected Poems: Fragments and Fictions* (Seren, 1988); for his translation of the Traditional Verse (Anon.) from *The Oxford Book of Welsh Verse in English* (Oxford University Press, 1973).

Gwyn Jones for his translation of the Traditional Verse (Anon.) from *The Oxford Book of Welsh Verse in English*, (Oxford University Press, 1973); for the extract from 'Shacki Thomas' from *The Buttercup Field* (Penmark Press, 1945); and for his co-translation (with Thomas Jones) of the extracts from *The Mabinogion* (J.M. Dent & Sons, 1989).

Mair Jones for the estate of Thomas Jones for his co-translation (with Gwyn Jones) of extracts from *The Mabinogion* (J.M. Dent & Sons, 1989).

Sally Roberts Jones for 'Moving House Again' from *The Forgotten Country* and 'Turning Away' from *Turning Away* (Gomer, 1969).

The estate of Alun Lewis for permission to reprint 'A War Wedding' and 'Post-script: for Gweno' from *Raiders' Dawn* (Allen and Unwin, 1942); 'Goodbye' from *Ha! Ha! Among the Trumpets* (Allen and Unwin, 1945); 'Acting Captain' from *The Last Inspection* (Allen and Unwin, 1943) and *Collected Stories* (Seren, 1990).

Michael Joseph Ltd. and Susan H. Llewellyn for the Estate of Richard Llewellyn for the extract from *How Green was my Valley* (1939).

Hilary Llewellyn-Williams for 'Life Class' from *Book of Shadows* (Seren, 1990).

The Estate of David Lloyd George for extracts from *My Darling Pussy: The Letters of Lloyd George and Frances Stevenson, 1913-41,* edited by A.J.P. Taylor (Weidenfeld and Nicolson, 1975).

Christopher Meredith for permission to reprint the extract from his novel, *Shifts* (Seren, 1988).

Robert Minhinnick for 'A Term of Pan' from *A Thread in the Maze* (Christopher Davies, 1978).

Leslie Norris for 'Hudson's Geese' from *A Sea in the Desert* (Seren, 1989).

The estate of John Ormond for 'To a Nun', 'Design for a Quilt' and 'In September' from *Selected Poems* (Seren, 1987).

Philip Owens for 'Spring Wedding', originally published in *Poetry Wales*.

Alan Perry for 'Marlene' and 'Watering the Flowers' both from *Fires on the Common* (Christopher Davies, 1975).

Richard Poole for 'Separation' from *Madog*, Vol.2, No. 2, and *Words Before Midnight* (Poetry Wales Press, 1981).

Sheenagh Pugh for 'Outside the Registry Office' from *Crowded by Shadows* (Christopher Davies, 1977) and 'Spring' originally published in *Poetry Wales*. Both poems available in her *Selected Poems* (Seren, 1990).

Andre Deutsch Ltd., for the Estate of Jean Rhys for permission to reprint extracts from *Smile Please* (Andre Deutsch, 1979) and *Voyage in the Dark* (Constable, 1934, re-issued in 1967 by Andre Deutsch).

Alun Richards for permission to reprint 'The Scandalous Thoughts of Elmyra Mouth' from *Dai Country*, (Michael Joseph, 1976); and 'Jehoidah's Gents' from *The Former Miss Merthyr Tydfil & Other Stories*, (Michael Joseph, 1973). Both stories were re-printed in Penguin's edition of his *Collected Stories* in 1978.

Lynette Roberts for 'Poem from Llanybri' from *Poems* (Faber, 1944).

Meic Stephens for 'The Owl', first published in the *Anglo-Welsh Review* and included in his booklet *Exiles All* (Christopher Davies, 1973).

David Higham Associates for the Estate of Dylan Thomas for 'When all my Five and Country Senses See', and 'Light Breaks where no Sun Shines' from *The Poems*; for the included selections from *Under Milk Wood*; for the extracts of 'Extraordinary Little Cough' and 'One Warm Saturday' from *Portrait of the Artist as a Young Dog*; and for the extract from *A Prospect of the Sea*.

Jeffrey Robinson for the estate of Gwyn Thomas for permission to reprint an extract from *The Alone to the Alone* (Nicholson & Watson Ltd. 1947).

R.S. Thomas for: (an extract from) *The Minister* (Montgomeryshire Printing Co., Newtown, 1953); 'The Way of It' from *The Way of It* (Ceolfrith Press, Sunderland, 1977); 'Like That' from *Laboratories of the Spirit* (Macmillan, 1975); 'Madrigal' from *The Stones of The Field* (Druid Press, Carmarthen, 1946); and 'Strays' from *Later Poems* (Macmillan, 1983).

Jean Henderson for the Estate of John Tripp for 'My Courtship of Miss Roberts' from *The Province of Belief* (Christopher Davies, 1971) and 'Snap at Cold Knap 1938' from *The Loss of Ancestry* (Christopher Davies, 1969) and reprinted in *Selected Poems* (Seren, 1989).

John Powell Ward for 'The Imitation Burtons', originally published in *Poetry Wales*, also from *The Other Man* (Christopher Davies, 1969).

G.M. Watkins for the Estate of Vernon Watkins for 'Great Night's Returning' from *Cypress and Acacia* (Faber, 1959), also in *The Collected Poems of Vernon Watkins* (Golgonooza Press, 1985).

Herbert Williams for 'Perhaps', originally broadcast on BBC Radio.

AUTHOR INDEX

About the Editors

Siân James was born near Llandysul, Cardiganshire, and educated at Aberystwyth. She is the author of nine novels, including *A Small Country*, *Storm at Arberth* and *Love & War*, and has twice won the Yorkshire Post Prize for Fiction. She now lives in Warwickshire.

Tony Curtis has written nine collections of poetry, most recently *Heaven's Gate*. He has edited a number of anthologies and critical works, including *The Poetry of Pembrokeshire*, *The Poetry of Snowdonia* and *Coal*, and has published two volumes of interviews with Welsh artists. He is Professor of Poetry at the University of Glamorgan and a Fellow of the Royal Society of Literature.

Other anthologies from Seren you may enjoy

Letters from Wales edited by Joan Abse £14.95 hbk

Ranging over eight centuries, this fascinating anthology of private and public correspondence, journals and diary entries provides an enthralling commentary on Wales. From Kings, Princes and Bishops to writers, artists and politicians; from the medieval machinations of Glyndwr and Hotspur to bitter industrial disputes; from Oliver Cromwell to Lloyd George, George Eliot to Dylan Thomas: a richly textured, entertaining and informative book emerges.

Childhood edited by Dewi Roberts £9.99 pbk

Childhood has always been a source of particular fascination for writers. This hugely entertaining and wide-ranging anthology surveys the pleasures and pains of growing up. Here are our shared experiences of childhood – the everyday and the extraordinary – in poems, stories, novels and memoirs. These pieces are sure to strike a chord with grown-ups everywhere – and put them in touch with the child within. Includes Gwyn Thomas, Siân James, Francis Kilvert, Henry Vaughan, Glenda Beagan, Dylan Thomas, Kate Roberts, Robert Graves, Leslie Norris, Glyn Jones, Gillian Clarke, Dannie Abse, and many others.

Birdsong edited by Dewi Roberts £7.95 pbk

From the epic mythologies of the Mabinogion through to the present day, birds have exerted a powerful influence on the literature of Wales. This unique anthology brings together a remarkable range of poetry and prose, illustrating the varied and multi-layered responses of writers across the centuries. Fragile, yet marvellously enduring, birds are the spark for powerful writing, a cause of wonder, reverence and joyous celebration. Includes RS Thomas, Gerard Manley Hopkins, Gillian Clarke, Gwyneth Lewis, Dafydd ap Gwilym, William Condry and many more.

Christmas in Wales edited by Dewi Roberts £6.95 pbk

Celebrate Christmas the Welsh way, in the company of some of the country's leading writers, past and present. Among the many subjects drawn from stories, poems, diaries and letters are Christmas Mass, the Nativity Play, plum pudding and turkey, folk customs such as the Mari Lwyd, shopping, presents, frost and snow, and the post-Christmas blues. *Christmas in Wales* is the perfect literary companion to the festive season, a present that will be opened again and again...

www.seren-books.com